STAFFORDSHIRE

Edited by Dave Thomas

First published in Great Britain in 1999 by
POETRY NOW YOUNG WRITERS
Remus House,
Coltsfoot Drive,
Woodston,
Peterborough, PE2 9JX
Telephone (01733) 890066

HB ISBN 0 75431 472 3
SB ISBN 0 75431 473 1

FOREWORD

Poetry Now Young Writers have produced poetry books in conjunction with schools for over eight years; providing a platform for talented young people to shine. This year, the Celebration 2000 collection of regional anthologies were developed with the millennium in mind.

With the nation taking stock of how far we have come, and reflecting on what we want to achieve in the future, our anthologies give a vivid insight into the thoughts and experiences of the younger generation.

We were once again impressed with the quality and attention to detail of every entry received and hope you will enjoy the poems we have decided to feature in *Celebration 2000 Staffordshire* for many years to come.

CONTENTS

Amington Heath Primary School
Hayley Brocklehurst	1
Kirsty Clinton	1
Thomas Dawson	2
Nathan Diamond	2
Kaye Nolan	3
Alison Sellars	3
Robyn Young	4
Emma Taylor	4
Andrew Rowland	5
Kayte Dudley	5
Samantha Woolley	6
Jemma Yapp	6
Ben Priestly	6
Holly Homer	7
Lindsey Wheatley	7
Nicola Harper	8
Natalie Evans	8
Elizabeth Harris	9
Kyle Deacon	9
Jade Levi Dowie	10
Erkan Sayman	10

Boney Hay Primary School
Megan Herring	11
Stephen Mitchell	11
Rachel Howard	12
Spencer Burke	12
Christopher Faulkner	13
Rebecca Chance	13
Jamie Tatlow	14
Stuart Taylor	14
Thomas Wyke	14
Aaron Mobley	15

Holly Punnett 15
Adrian Saxon 16
Sam Lloyd-Jones 16
David Smith 16
Leanne Lennon 17
Robyn Jones 17
Abbie Price 18
Chantal Mau 18
Bradley Gutterige 19
Laura Jones 19

Bursley CP School

Bethany Newstead 19
Jenna Hallen 20
Joel Dacey 21
Daniel Timmis 21
Michael Frost 22
Kerry Warburton 23
Megan Griffiths 24
Laura Kelly 24
Katherine Johnson 25
Jenny Shaw 26
Heather Matthews 26
Adele Salt 27
Simon Hand & Daniel Green 28
Samantha Worrall 28
Jenny Potter 29
Amy Flanagan 30
Nicola Boote 30
Siobhan Hodgkinson 31
Daniel Sayers 31
Richard Blakemore 32
Lucy Gater 32
Sarah Dutton 33
Rachel Ballard 34
Alexander Garner 34
Gary Palmer 35

Samantha Holdcroft   36
Ashley Bagley   36
Larne Barlow   37
Michael Smith   37

Church Eaton Endowed (A) Primary School
Richard Hemmings   38
Faye Wrotchford   38
Sally-Anne Ashby   39
Katie Frost   40
Rebekah Herbert   40
Andrew Woodward   41
Frances Gibson   42
Richard Harper   42
Roxanne Hill   43
Rachel Massie   44
Charlotte Brown   45
Katy James   46
Thomas Beech   47

Doxey Primary School
Laura James   48
David Arkinstall   48
Natalie Williams   49
Sharon Johnson   50
Laura Whiting   50
Chelsea Pettigrew   51
Jodie Ashington   52
Anthony Knapp   52
Daniel Padley   53
Claire Whitehouse   53
Christine Gault   54
Michael Webber   55
Nathan Butlin   55
Janine Davies   56
Melissa Pople   56
Simmone Williams   57

Vicky Pattyson	58
Lauren Maple	59
Claire Gaisford	60
Caroline Moore	60

Greenacres Primary School

Ben Ashwood	61
Shane Morris	61
Rachael Bonas	62
Ben Diamond	62
Karen Dhaliwal	63
Matthew Wedge	64
James Brown	64
Chris Chapman	65
Kirsty Burford	66
Lucy Coles	66
Caroline Prince	67
Clint Wilson	67
Aimee Edwards	68
Bethany Wroe	69
Claire Whithouse	70
Joe Grimley	70
Ashley Gough	71
Lucy Shutt	72

Longwood County Primary School

Carl Baldwin	72
Jodie Withers	73
Luke Slater	73
Katie Tallis	74
Leanne Orton	74
Elizabeth Emery	75
Olivia Shepherd	75
Danielle Worrell	76
Sinead Langford	76
Kielea Woods	77

Shaun Cordell	77
Katie Stanley	78
Victoria Dubberley	78
Lisa Tooley	79

Needwood CE (A) Primary School

Sarah Kent	79
Catherine Walker	80
Jodie Baxter	81
Rebecca Roberts	82
Sam Murphy	82
Emma Preston	83
Guy Atkinson	84
Amy Bendall	85
Megan Atkinson	86

Newton Regis Primary School

Natasha Broadhurst	86
Tom Martin	87
Terri South	87
Clare Louise Jones	88
Rachel Gray	88
Grace Coverson	89

Oakridge Primary School

Hannah Wetton	89
Matthew Taylor	90
Milly Parkes	90
Alexander Dodd	91
Sarah Parkinson	92
Ryan Nokes	92
Hannah Hulme	93
Ceri Waltho	94
Emma Waldron	94
Sophie Barrett	95
Catherine Le Chevalier	96
Edward Wallbank	96

George Wilson	97
David Bowen	98
Sophie Knight	99

Peartree Primary School

Emma Ralls	99
Austin Lockett	100

St Christopher's RC Primary School, Codsall

Thomas Henry Lister	100
Kimberley Everitt	101
Kathryn Lampitt	101
Alexander Hatfield	102
Amy Eardly	102
James Hayes	103
Alexander Mullen-Jones	103
Annamaria Casa	104
Samantha Taylor	104
Robyn Hayley Morais	105
Jonathan Maley	105
Elizabeth Metcalfe	106
Roseanne Gee	106
Jack O'Donovan	107
Jamie Halliwell	107
Joseph Hill	108
Alastair Mason	108
Siobhan Fern-Feeney	109
Joanne Ledder	109
William Blacker	110
Edward Evans	110
Omoregie Nehikhare	111
Thomas Griffin	111
Will D'Costa	112
Liam Kilbane	112
Edward Rogers	113
James Davies	114
Kaleigh Diver	114
Lauren Kavanagh	115

Matthew Acton   116
Hannah O'Shea   117
Rose Lister   117
Iain Olliver   118
Thomas Beavon   118
Sarah Stowe   119
Emma Dunn   119
Victoria Hargrove   120
Matthew Kulyna   120
Laura Peacock   121
Stephen Olliver   122
Joseph Thompson   122
Laura Moss   123
Lyndsey Denning   124
Emma Acton   124
Katherine Aston   125
Emma Davies   126
James Turner   127
Vikki Brown   128
Rachael Sharples   128
Victoria Marie Dunn   129
Elizabeth Handley   130

St John's CE Primary Schook, Stafford
Kyla Worrall   130
Rhian Parry   131
Vicky Ann Pickford   131
Kiran Madzimbamuto-Ray   132
Hannah Crossett   132
James Duckworth   133
Kerry Tutty   133
Scott Weetch   134
Emma Ludlow   134
Alex Sandford   135
Vanessa Youlden   135
Natalie Harrop   136
Daniel Boulten   136
William Riley-Gibson   137

Jamie Tindall 137
Idean Farshbaf 138
Jemma Finlay 138
Emily Clapham 139
Leona Jones-Keating 139
James Hodson 140
Sahar Shahid Nadeem 140
Helen Dean 141
Danielle Bridgland 141
Sarah Rizeq 142
Andrew Gallear 143
Kyle James Smith 143
Megan Preece 144
Damon Morbey 145
Joshua Baker 145
Emma Jane Siggery 146
Jack Davis 146
Christopher Fox 147
Samantha Butt 147
Louise Brandrick 147
Deven Morton 148
Ben Fleming 148
Joe Murray 149
Liz Howard 149
David Bufton 150
Kathryn Brophy 150
Rachel Cawley 151
Victoria Philp 151
Sarah Woodward 152
Lindsey Walkeden 152
Hannah Clark 153
Richard Cropper 153
Andy Pringle 154
James Ludlow 154
Andrew Oldham 155
Holly Buckless 155
Scott Haley 156
Kim Rushworth 157

Donna Owen	157
Peter Whyman	157
Matthew Tyzack	158
Gurdev Gill	158
Philippa Wimpory	159
Michael Jones	159
Sally Ecclestone	160
Emily Swales	160
Robert Fowler	161
Rebecca Revell	161
Holly Dunkley	162
Darryll Johns	162
Matthew Gollins	163
Scott Roebuck	163
Nicholas Sandiford	163
Rachel Lawson	164
Sarah Healy	164
Jodie Warner	165
Robert Reading	165
Scott Randles	166
Peter Jones	166
Laura Teitge	166
Kate Bufton	167
Luke Mudford	168
Robert Senior	168
Lorna Perry	169
Matthew Suffolk	169
Patrick Durie	170
Seonaid Fleming	170

St Joseph & St Theresa's RC Primary School, Burntwood

Darren Rogers	171
Dominic Parsons	171
Kyle Ball	172
Darren Hames	172
Rebecca Ward	173
Andrea Jagielski	173
Kimberley Rogers	174

Luke Service	174
Aiden McNamara	175
Amy Wicks	175
Jason Upton	176
Kristine Chandler	176
James Pearson	177
Victoria Anne Smith	177
Jennifer Ralphs	178
Sofie Leroux	178
Jordan Blake	179

St Margaret's CE Junior School, Newcastle-under-Lyme

Caitlin Grainger	180
Jessica Ann Crooks	180
Stephen Jackson	181
Richard Simpson	181
Matthew Fernyhough	182
Jennifer Maddock	182
Rachel Hancock	183
Rebecca Goddard	183
Katie Stanway	184
Kate Tarpey	184
Stevie Saponja	185
Amber Allen	185
Charlotte Kerr	186
Lauren Bailey	186
Eve Funnell	187
Phoebe Sparrow	187
Emily Worrall	188
Leanne Ray	188
Duncan McNeil	189
Lee Hughes	189
Amy Johnson	190
Matthew Cotton	190
Emma Walker	191
Stephen Barrs	191
Lucy S Street	192
Rachel Millward	192

Alex Pardoe 193
Gregory Braddick 193
Daniel Parker 194
Stuart Kelly 194
Philip Jolley 195
Laura Burgess 196
Sophie Wood 197
Alexandra Powney 197
Charlotte Weller 198
Janine Larkin 199
Iain Hope 199
Bruce Halliwell 200
Sam Massey 200
Anthony Zobkiw 200
Toby Plant 201

St Mary's RC Primary School, Leek
Robert Standell 202
Tawny Hill 203
Vu Anh Nguyen 203
Emma Carter 204
Benjamin Field 204
Samuel Henry Hunt 204
Elizabeth Sillito 205
Cassie Bratt 206
Anna Niebieska 206

St Thomas's RC Primary School, Tean,
Lorna Poole, Elisa Etemad,
Christina Wallace, Abigail Hall
& Marianne King 207
Alex Humphries 207
Lee Wood, John Finnegan, Dale Tunstall,
Liam Forristal & Grant Ravenscroft 208
Oonagh Scannell, Amy Burgoyne,
Natasha Hallam, Judith Downie
& Luke Dalkin 208

Sophie Whieldon, Caroline Darley,
Mark Mogadam, Jessica Darley,
& Emma Walford   209
Yan Pavlovic, Robert Smith,
Samuel Worthington, Kristian Finney
& Adam Layland   210
Laura Marsh, Heather Deaville,
Kirsty Shotton, Kelly Rushton,
& Lindsay Withington   210

Springvale County Primary School

Megan Wilson	211
Richard Woolley	211
Natasha Wilton	212
Joseph Apperley	212
Natalie Jones	213
James Poynton	213
Lauren Butler	214
Adam Heath	214
Kristina Fisher	215
Terri Lea Bentley	215
Julian Bishop	216
Lisa Bate	216
Adam Penhorwood	216
Alfie Poynton	217

Stoneydelph Junior School

Rebecca Bishop	217

Tillington Manor Primary School

Lauren Johnston	218
Scott Hall	219
Soibhian Knight	219
Jamie Cartwright	220

William Shrewsbury Primary School

Aaron Nixon	220
Michael Duddy	221
Johnathan Armstrong	221
Charlotte Nutland	222
Jamie Sandells	223
Ben Watson	223
Sophie Horner	224
Stacey Smith	224
Andrew Lamb	224
Sophie Partridge	225

The Poems

CELEBRATION 2000

It is New Year's,
So get up and dance,
It will never end,
With laughter and fun.

So come on boogie,
Poppers go *bang!*
Millennium time.

With music and dance,
And people that sing,
So come on boogie,
It's nearly new year.

Hayley Brocklehurst (9)
Amington Heath Primary School

CELEBRATION 2000

The new year is here,
And everyone's drinking beer,
For the celebration is so dear,
It goes so fast,
And it's going to last,
Some go to nightclubs,
Some stay at home,
Some are so excited,
They all go to bed,
And wait till January 1st.

Kirsty Clinton (10)
Amington Heath Primary School

CELEBRATION 2000

Can you hear the fireworks going,
Can you hear the strong winds blowing,
Can you hear us all celebrating,
Can you hear an old man shouting?
I'm watching the people on the rides,
Especially the people on the slides,
They come down zooming so fast,
And when they get down they exclaim 'At last,'
Year 2000 is here,
And everybody's got a tear.

There was a firework like a bottle,
That took off like a shuttle,
One shot off and exploded into a picture of a UFO,
Another one shot off and looked like a bow,
And this is the end of the night,
Of our really scary fright.

Thomas Dawson (10)
Amington Heath Primary School

CELEBRATION 2000

Celebrating New Year's
It is nearly here,
It's a brand new year,
Be careful of your beer,
It is really here,
It is a millennium,
It's surely an important year.

Nathan Diamond (10)
Amington Heath Primary School

CELEBRATION 2000

We will all gather on this special day,
To see all the fireworks whizzing away,
We all go on rides and shout hip, hip, hooray,
It should turn out to be a wonderful day,
Let's get all of the family around,
Let's get the Millennium band,
Let's clap our hands to the beat,
And even tap our feet,
Let's get back to the fireworks before the night ends,
The very last firework suddenly sounds,
I watched the route of it fall to the ground,
That was the end of the millennium I found.

Kaye Nolan (10)
Amington Heath Primary School

CELEBRATION 2000

We celebrate the year 2000
And play lots of games
And the year 2000
Will bring parties back again
In the year 2000 we will have fireworks

We celebrate the year 2000
And have big parties
People go to the Millennium Dome
After a bit they all go home
And they do have lots of cakes
But not the children, it's all for me

Alison Sellars (9)
Amington Heath Primary School

THE YEAR 2000

I'm going to a party,
I'm going on holiday,
It's the year 2000!
Celebration year 2000!
Let's go to a party!
Let's go on holiday.

We're going to the Millennium Dome,
We're gonna dance all night,
It's the year 2000!
Celebration 2000!
Let's go to the Millennium Dome!
Let's dance all night!

We'll stay up late,
We'll see the New Year,
It's the year 2000!
Celebration 2000!
Let's stay up late,
Let's see the New Year.

Robyn Young (9)
Amington Heath Primary School

CELEBRATION 2000

Celebration, celebration for 2000,
Millennium is here,
So let's dance all night.
Let's look, go outside and watch the fireworks dance,
Because the millennium is here.

Emma Taylor (10)
Amington Heath Primary School

CELEBRATION 2000

10 days till the millennium,
Come gather round we'll have a celebration,
There we'll have food, drink and famous people,
So now we've had an invitation,
Come because it will be excellent.

Let's all bring food so we can give it to the poor people,
And then we would all be kind,
Just like Jesus would, but,
Still come and have a celebration.

Think of the places we can invent,
Think of the places we can visit,
Just like the Millennium Dome.

Andrew Rowland (10)
Amington Heath Primary School

CELEBRATION 2000

It is coming at last,
Don't look to the past,
Today we go party
Everyone's coming.
We'll dance all night,
It will be alright,
No worries today,
So let's shout hooray!
Hooray! Hooray!

Kayte Dudley (9)
Amington Heath Primary School

CELEBRATION 2000

We have all been living for 2000 years,
Let's have a big party and dance the night away,
People drink lots of beer,
This is a special day to cheer,
Lets celebrate for the Millennium,
Lets get the street to party!
Party, party, Millennium!

Samantha Woolley (10)
Amington Heath Primary School

CELEBRATION 2000

Millennium millennium Robbie Williams will be pleased,
Millennium millennium no-one knows what it will bring,
Millennium millennium parties round the corner.
Millennium millennium watch the fireworks and laughter.

Jemma Yapp (11)
Amington Heath Primary School

CELEBRATION 2000

Celebration, celebration
You have come today
Me and my friends have gone out to play
The year 2000 has come today.

Ben Priestly (9)
Amington Heath Primary School

CELEBRATION 2000

The two thousand's coming,
And everyone's humming,
Let's go to dance,
And see some romance,
Yes it's coming and it's humming, it's coming, it's coming.

Hear the fireworks, hear the bangers,
Bang, pop, hear them scare you,
So when they pop and when they bang,
I hear everyone sing,
Yes it's coming and it's humming, it's coming, it's coming.

So come on, see the fun,
And in the morning hopefully out will come the sun,
We'll never see it again,
So enjoy yourself,
And don't be so sad.

Holly Homer (10)
Amington Heath Primary School

CELEBRATION 2000

The millennium has come today
I always come out to play
I shout all round hooray, hooray
The year 2000 has come today.

I wander around screaming and shouting
To say the millennium has come today, today, today
The millennium has come today.

Lindsey Wheatley (11)
Amington Heath Primary School

CELEBRATION 2000

A million years is at an end,
It is the year 2000 my friend.
We're gonna have a party for the years gone by,
Until the sun rises in the sky!

But there is sadness everywhere,
Because all them years have gone
Forever when the clock says 12.01.
Your guests have gone home,
You're left
All
Alone
In your home
Covered with party poppers that went *bang!!!*
Your husband speaks, then it is clear.
He says
'It's a chance to start again . . .
My dear.'

Nicola Harper (11)
Amington Heath Primary School

CELEBRATION 2000

The year 2000 has come today
All the children have come out to play
We all shout 'Hooray Hooray'
The Millennium has come today
Friends, families and all such more
Come along and knock on the door
Party poppers on the floor
'Please go, I don't want anymore!'

Natalie Evans (11)
Amington Heath Primary School

CELEBRATION OF THE YEAR 2000

This year to celebrate
The new millennium
I'm going down to my Grandma's
We're going down to Cornwall
We will go to the beach
It's the year 2000
Celebrate the year 2000.

The millennium's just beginning
The bells will be ringing
There will be fun
There will be laughter
And we will live
Happily ever after
In the
Millennium.

Elizabeth Harris (10)
Amington Heath Primary School

CELEBRATION 2000

The Millennium is coming,
Everyone is excited,
Everyone is partying, rockin' and rollin' around the street,
Running around jumping and screaming,
The Millennium has come,
Fireworks flying through the air,
Bang!
Bang!
Bang!
This day will be remembered,
By everyone.

Kyle Deacon (11)
Amington Heath Primary School

CELEBRATION 2000

The millennium is here,
Parties everywhere,
Fireworks are crackling,
Fireworks are shooting,
People here and there,
Everybody celebrate, celebrate, celebrate!

Party poppers are banging,
People are having fun,
Fair ride bells are ringing,
Everyone is singing,
So celebrate, celebrate, celebrate!

There goes another firework going,
The trumpets, trombones and horns blowing,
There's another blowing horn,
It's been 2000 years since Jesus was born!
So everybody celebrate, celebrate, celebrate!

Jade Levi Dowie (9)
Amington Heath Primary School

CELEBRATION 2000

Find the fireworks in the sky,
Find a way to start the day,
People are coming so they start drumming,
For the millennium.
I can't wait to start the play,
Look inside to find the time,
We are always here so stop your tear,
We'll never have a fear.

Erkan Sayman (9)
Amington Heath Primary School

THE BUTTERFLY

I was a chrysalis once
I was so safe
But now I have grown up.

I was a caterpillar once
I was all green
But now I have grown up.

I have wings of all pretty colours
Red, yellow, blue, green and purple.

I can fly way up high
In the blue, blue sky.

I was a butterfly once!

Megan Herring (9)
Boney Hay Primary School

THE LEOPARD

The leopard runs through the jungle,
He creeps up on his prey, then he's off in a dash,
He kills with one paw,
Then he eats in a flash.

He has lots of spots,
Like a child with chickenpox.
He hides in the grass so you don't know he's passed.

Stephen Mitchell (8)
Boney Hay Primary School

THE CAT

Cats are furry
thin and warm,
Cats have whiskers
black and tickly,
Cats have tails
long and curly,
Cats chase mice,
eat fishy spice,
Cats pull wool,
very playful,
Cats are fun
messing with Mum.

Rachel Howard (8)
Boney Hay Primary School

SNOWY OWL

Gliding through the night,
Silent winged,
Hunting too,
Eyes sparkle like stars,
Observant stare,
Prey to attack,
Swooping suddenly down,
Claws opened,
Prey caught.

Spencer Burke (9)
Boney Hay Primary School

THE GIRAFFE

His neck is tall,
Not very fat at all,
Ears are very small,
With spots orange and yellow,
He's a big old fellow,
That lives in the jungle.

There are dots and plenty of spots,
All living together on his back,
He's big like a multi-storey block
It would be good living on a giraffe's back,
With spots orange and yellow,
He's a big old fellow,
That lives in the jungle.

Christopher Faulkner (9)
Boney Hay Primary School

AUNT NELLY

My Aunt Nelly watches telly,
With her hands on her belly,
And her feet on a stool.

My Aunt Nelly is very very smelly,
In her old red welly,
And her feet on a stool.

My Aunt Nelly eats strawberry jelly,
From her other smelly welly,
With her feet on a stool.

Rebecca Chance (8)
Boney Hay Primary School

THE SNOWY OWL

The snowy owl
Wings spread like a kite.
He flaps his wings like a kite,
Looking for food in the night.
Snowy flappy like a kite,
His eyes are shining in the night.

Jamie Tatlow (8)
Boney Hay Primary School

THE RATTLESNAKE

The rattlesnake has a mighty rattle!
It's very big and scary,
It lies in a den all day,
So we'd better be wary,
The rattlesnake has a mighty rattle!

Stuart Taylor (9)
Boney Hay Primary School

THE OWL

Silent and swift
Swoops in the sky
Suddenly appearing
Scared prey caught

Thomas Wyke (9)
Boney Hay Primary School

BARN OWLS

Owls at night,
Ready for a fight,
Swooping down looking for a bite,
Prey on the ground,
Nabs it with a bound,
Takes it to the chicks,
Lies it in the sticks,
Swallows it whole,
Like water going down a hole,
Lies down for a rest,
Safely in the nest.

Aaron Mobley (9)
Boney Hay Primary School

GUESS THE ANIMAL

This animal is rather big,
It has very sharp claws and beak,
It likes to go out and catch its food at night,
It has big round eyes to see in the night,
And it makes a sound like this . . .
Tu-whit tu-whoo,
If you have not guessed yet,
I'll have to tell you now,
It's an
Owl.

Holly Punnett (9)
Boney Hay Primary School

My Rabbit

My cute little rabbit,
Is small and furry,
He likes to sleep not hurry.

When he comes out for his daily run,
He goes under the shed to hide from the sun,
When we call him he does come.

Adrian Saxon (8)
Boney Hay Primary School

The Snake

The slow snake slides along the ground
hunting for his prey,
The slow snake hides behind a rock
waiting for his prey,
The slow snake strikes and bites his meal
thankful for his prey.

Sam Lloyd-Jones (8)
Boney hay Primary School

The Black Spiders

Spiders, spiders small and fat,
Spiders, spiders black and hairy,
Spiders, spiders eating other insects on the wall,
Spiders, spiders catching greenflies in webs,
Spiders, spiders without any necks.

David Smith (9)
Boney Hay Primary School

THE SLIPPERY SLIMY SNAKE

Slippery slimy snake
As thin as a flake

Slipping on the ground
Wonder if he's poisoned?

Sliding sluggishly
Slither, slithering, slithery

Smooth, silky snake
Swimming in the lake

Leanne Lennon (9)
Boney Hay Primary School

THE SLIPPERY SLIMY SNAKE

The slippery
Slimy snake,
Moved slowly
Through the lake.

The smooth
Slim snake,
Was as little
As a *thistle!*

Robyn Jones (9)
Boney Hay Primary School

SNAKES

Snakes have sharp teeth,
rather like a shark.
They have dozens of scales,
just like a hard shell.

Snakes feel really cold,
They smell with their tongue,
And eat the head's first,
Of their prey.

Snakes feel very smooth,
just like a stone.
When they're ready to attack,
Their body strikes up *sss.*

Some snakes can be wild,
and thin like a finger.
Some can be fat
and squeeze like a belt.

If the room is hot the snake's
blood is hot.
If the room is cold the snake's
blood is cold.

Abbie Price (9)
Boney Hay Primary School

DOLPHIN

He leaps through the water,
A shimmering sight,
His name is Flipper,
He calls at night.

Chantal Mau (8)
Boney Hay Primary School

GUESS WHAT!

Slide along the soil
Curl up in a coil
Search for some prey
Sleep night and day
Attack and kill with force
They are snakes of course!

Bradley Gutterige (8)
Boney Hay Primary School

POLLUTION OF THE WORLD

Destruction of my world has done this:
Water grubby polluted waste,
Car fumes contaminate the air,
Car fumes kill off the animals in the street and park,
Man has destroyed the road and it's difficult to live.

Laura Jones (9)
Boney Hay Primary School

THE GHOSTLY RIDER

The wind was a staring face,
The moon was a thick long lace,
The road was a squeaking mouse,
And the ghost rider came riding,
Riding, riding,
And the ghost rider came riding up to the haunted house.

Bethany Newstead (10)
Bursley CP School

MY MORNING

I woke up this morning
And found I was late,
So I ran downstairs
And opened the gate.

I woke up this morning
What a disaster,
I looked out of the window
And saw my headmaster.

I woke up this morning
All cheerful and bright,
The only problem was -
It wasn't light!

I woke up this morning
I couldn't believe,
The amount of tissues
Up my sleeve!

I woke up this morning
At ten-past eight,
And to my surprise,
I wasn't late!

I woke up this morning
And to my surprise,
I found that I couldn't
Open my eyes!

I woke up this morning
And what do you know?
I looked through the window
And there was the snow!

Jenna Hallen (10)
Bursley CP School

I HATE HURRICANES

I hate hurricanes,
They crash and smash,
Tidal wave,
Splash,
Gurgle,
Screaming,
Hurricanes are fearless,
And evil,
The hurricane,
Has no mercy,
It just wants to,
Destroy.

Joel Dacey (11)
Bursley CP School

THE STRANGE HOUSE

I walked in the garden
And someone said pardon.
I went in the house
And saw a strange mouse.
I went in the living room
And saw a witch on a broom.
I went upstairs
Slipping on hairs.
I looked at the bath
And heard a laugh.
I thought . . . what a strange house!

Daniel Timmis
Bursley CP School

THE MONSTROUS MONSTER

In the cave that no one's found,
You're right, it's far away!
In the day, it's quite dark,
In the night, it's day.

In the cave that no one's found,
A monster lives within!
And if you're brave and in you go,
You'll see his next of kin.

In the cave that no one's found,
The monster is ugly now -
And when his tea time slowly comes,
His food is a big cow.

In the cave that no one's found,
The monster looks like this,
His head is big, his eyes are small,
His lips they want to kiss.

In the cave that no one's found,
The monster makes a massive sound,
And when you look at his big ears,
You fall right to the ground.

In the cave that no one's found,
You're right, it's far away!
In the day, it's quite dark,
In the night, it's day.

In the cave that no one's found,
Inside a monster hides,
Now you've heard this description,
Perhaps you'll stay inside!

Michael Frost (9)
Bursley CP School

TEA

Busy day,
Working, listening,
Home time's near,
Eyes start glistening.

The bell rings loud,
Children running,
Dan wants a fight,
He looks cunning.

Want my tea,
Waiting, waiting,
Knock at the door,
Friends are dating.

Mum calls,
Nose sniffing,
Run inside,
Forks lifting.

Open wide,
Down it goes,
Yum, yum,
Mouth close.

Want more,
Chomp, swallow,
Disappears,
Lots follow.

Pudding comes,
Wobbly jelly,
Where's it gone?
In my belly.

Kerry Warburton (10)
Bursley CP School

THE HUMBLIES

They went to space on a spoon they did,
On a spoon they went to space,
In spite of all their sisters could say,
On a sunny morn', on a winter's day,
On a spoon they went to space!

And when the spoon carried them far away,
And everyone cried 'It's almost May,'
They called aloud, 'The time can pass,
But we don't mind, we might land on grass.'

On a spoon we'll go to space!
Far and few, far and few,
Are the lands where the Humblies live,
Their eyes are black, their tongues are blue,
And they went to space on a spoon.

Megan Griffiths (9)
Bursley CP School

MY SPECIAL PLACE

I walked silently up my garden,
On a cold winter's day,
I crept up on my steps,
While my cat passed by.

I walked silently up my path,
Looking at all the snow on the flowers,
I was wondering what to do,
Then suddenly I ran into the shed.

I walked silently on to my grass,
To pick a lovely flower,
I knocked off all the snow,
And watched it melt.

I walked silently down my steps,
Then suddenly heard a mouse creep past,
My cat ran after it,
And tossed it to and fro.

Laura Kelly (10)
Bursley CP School

SEASONS

W hite crystals lie on the ground,
I   cicles hang from frost covered roofs,
N   ow the winter is here, there are diamonds everywhere,
T   here are ice-lollies in my gloves,
E   merald grass peeps out of the quilt of snow,
R   obins huddle up in the bare branches of trees.

S   un's rays spread out to give light and gleam, through the pink
     blossom trees.
U nder trees, bees drift round each jewelled flower,
M eanwhile up in the air butterflies fly about, looking down at the
     glittering ponds,
M ornings are cool and breezy with the sun shining on the emerald
     grass.
E   arly in the mornings there are glassy drops of dew,
R   obins sing merrily in the green treetops.

Katherine Johnson (9)
Bursley CP School

SEASONS

White frost sprinkled on the ground like sweet sugar,
Icicles hang off every white crystal roof,
Noses nibbled, red and sore every night and day,
The wind whistles a high pitched noise
Through the bare trees,
Emerald grass peeks out of a blanket of snow,
Ribbons of smoke drift through a sapphire sky.

Sun's rays gleam through blossom trees,
Underground insects scuttle in their nests,
Morning's bright whisper that the day is kind,
My hair blows in the warm breeze,
Evergreen trees are bright and blooming,
Red roses spread out like colourful peacock feathers.

Jenny Shaw (9)
Bursley CP School

THE MONSTER

In a dark and deep dishevelled cave,
There's someone waiting to dispute your grave,
And don't endure the pain of death,
He's waiting for you with his one eyed head,
And he'll kill you in your safe warm bed.

His claws will come out and you he'll grab,
And if you're not careful it's your mind he'll stab,
You'll never forget his fierce red eyes,
So stay under the blanket, safe, if you're wise,
And muffle the sound of your scared howling cries.
Remember he's only a dream of your mind!

Heather Matthews (10)
Bursley CP School

ONE BUSY SCHOOL DAY

My clock rings, I wake up,
The doorbell dings,
My mum passes me a drink of tea,
In a china cup.

I get my bag, the postman comes,
My brother off sick,
Is playing on his metal drums,
And there's my mum, *nag, nag, nag,*

At school, the bell rings,
Starting maths,
Finish maths,
All out.

After playtime, English starts,
Punctuation, adjectives, spelling test,
Twenty out of twenty,
Dinner time, dinner time, dinner time.

For my dinner I have,
Chips, pie, peas, gravy,
Apple crumble, custard and juice,
It is delicious.

At playtime I play,
Skipping, chasing, running, racing,
It is brilliant.

The afternoon goes quickly,
And soon it is home time,
I watch telly,
Have my tea,
Including jelly,
Then I go to bed,
To get ready for another busy school day.

Adele Salt (11)
Bursley CP School

Rainbow

*R*unning in the park
        suddenly it began to rain

*A*nd then I saw a seven
        colour ribbon bending in the sky

I saw a ruby red
        as bright as a brain

*N*ow I see an aqua orange
        learning how to fly

*B*rilliant violet went flashing
        past the corner of my eyes

*O*ne colour stood out so brightly
        it was the Indian indigo

*W*ow what a beautiful seven
        coloured ribbon that was that shot across the sky

Simon Hand (8) & Daniel Green (8)
Bursley CP School

Things We Have In Common

Said the little girl, 'Sometimes I fall off my chair.'
Said the lady, 'Sometimes I cut my hair.'
The little girl whispered,
'Sometimes I wear my underwear.'
And the lady whispered,
'Sometimes I cuddle my teddy bear.'
'I do that too,' giggled the little girl.
The lady said, 'I sometimes watch my coffee swirl.'
The little girl nodded, 'So do I.'

Samantha Worrall (11)
Bursley CP School

SCHOOL DINNERS

School dinners,
will never be winners,
at my school any day.
The trouble is you have to pay,
for all the scraps you throw away.

Monday it's
pies and over-done fries,
scalding hot mustard
and freezing cold custard.

Tuesday it's
frozen fishcakes
and a meat and potato oven-bake,
and for pud . . .
a plate full of mud!

Wednesday it's
bangers and mash,
served on the plate as quick as a flash,
not to mention the sloppy trifle.

Thursday it's
jacket potato, cheese and beans,
when you sleep they give you bad dreams.
For pudding there's crumbling shortcake,
so for goodness sake give me a break.

Friday it's
one piece of skinny turkey,
that looks sort of grey and murky,
to go with the rock solid peaches.

Jenny Potter (11)
Bursley CP School

THE PARK

My favourite place is the playground,
Where the trees blow in the wind,
Where children play all day long,
And flowers dance all day long.
Little children dance and sing,
And boys and girls play on the swing.

I love the park, I do, I do,
Especially when my friends are there too.
When the sun shines bright like fire,
It feels like I am on an aeroplane swishing through the sky.

The park is the best place I've ever been,
Where children play all day long,
And the stream that goes by, under the trees.
I wish I was in the park now,
Playing on the slide and swings.

Amy Flanagan (11)
Bursley CP School

THE FOREST

The wind blows between the trees,
   Gathering up the misty breeze.

It blew the flowers to and fro,
   Not knowing which way the stems will flow.

Even though the sun is bright,
   We may be heading for a stormy night.

Nicola Boote (11)
Bursley CP School

ONCE THERE WAS A LORRY

Once there was a lorry,
A ghostly lorry,
An extremely ghostly lorry,
And on that lorry,
There was a box,
A rusty box,
A weird rusty box,
And in that box,
There was a key,
A silver key,
And by that key,
There was a note,
An interesting note,
An incredibly interesting note,
And on that note there was a message,
A creepy message,
A strange creepy message,
Which grabbed my attention.

Siobhan Hodgkinson (11)
Bursley CP School

THE HOWLER

The wind was a swirling, winding wave.
The moon was a rocky, craggy cave.
The road was the twisting tail of a silver mouse,
And the howler came riding,
Riding, riding,
The howler came riding up to the haunted house.

Daniel Sayers (10)
Bursley CP School

ONCE THERE WAS A LORRY

Once there was a lorry,
A battered lorry,
A really battered lorry.
Inside that lorry
There was a crate,
An open crate,
A forced open crate,
By that crate
There was a message,
A scary message,
A very scary message,
Which brought me to the
Creature!

Richard Blakemore (11)
Bursley CP School

ALL ALONE

Pretty Girl,
All alone,
Nobody cared, she was on her own.
Nobody listened,
Nobody helped,
The little girl who walked about.
Up and down she always went,
Trying to find her mother's scent,
Hoping one day she would find,
Somebody who cared deep inside.
So she was left alone to find,
Somebody who cared, and was kind.

Lucy Gater (11)
Bursley CP School

OLD AND NEW

I suppose that
My special place
Is where I miss the most;
The coloured books,
The unpleasant pink,
That often comforted me.
The jam-packed desk,
The cluttered floor,
The posters old and new,
The old warn carpet
The bold TV cables
The curtains that didn't match.
But then it all changed,
I suppose
For the better . . .
Builders arrived!
They're banging and clanging,
Dirt and dust,
Then paint and carpet,
Curtains and bed clothes
And finally . . .
A brand new room,
Yellow and blue,
Bright and bold,
When the lights go out,
Stars and moons,
Suns and comets.
So here I lie
Looking around my room
Enjoying the features . . .
And . . .
The matching curtains!

Sarah Dutton (11)
Bursley CP School

ONCE THERE WAS A LORRY

Once there was a lorry,
A rusty lorry,
A rusty battered lorry,
And on that lorry
There was a box,
A little box,
A little old box
And in that box
There was a key,
A gold key,
A shiny gold key
And by that key
There was a note,
A scribbled note,
A quickly scribbled note
And on that note
There was a message,
An enormous message,
A scary enormous message
Which drew me to attention.

Rachel Ballard (11)
Bursley CP School

DISCO

On Friday 5th, the disco is ready
Come on boys keep the beat steady,
Steady, steady, because the disco's ready.

Everyone's dancing in the light
Everyone's dancing all the night,
Night, night, in the light.

Then there broke out a fight
In the glow of the light,
Light, light, there broke out a fight.

On Friday 5th, the disco has finished
Come on boys pack up the dishes
Dishes, dishes, because the disco's finished.

Alexander Garner (11)
Bursley CP School

ONCE THERE WAS A LORRY

Once there was a lorry,
A dented lorry,
A large dented lorry,
And on that lorry,
There was a box,
A small box,
A splintered small box,
And in that box,
There was a key,
A tiny rusty key,
And by that key,
There was a note,
A drenched wet note,
And on that note,
There was a message,
A frightening message,
Which drew me to danger.

Gary Palmer (10)
Bursley CP School

I'M MUCH BETTER THAN YOU!

My teacher's funnier than your teacher,
Got more children too.
My school is larger than your school,
I'm much better than you!

My bike's faster than your bike,
Our family is noisier too.
We have a house with a steam room,
I'm much better than you!

My TV cost more than your TV,
My shoes are shinier too.
My PC's worth more than your PC,
I'm much better than you!

My dog barks louder than your dog,
He's much cleaner too.
My little sister knows the alphabet,
I'm much better than you!

Samantha Holdcroft (10)
Bursley CP School

THE COWBOY

The wind was blowing faster than a fox's pace,
The moon was like a staring wide face.
The road was as long as the month of June,
And the cowboy came riding,
Riding, riding,
The cowboy came riding up to the old wooden-doored saloon.

Ashley Bagley (10)
Bursley CP School

THE MONSTER

His face is black like a dark, deep night,
He creeps about in the thin moonlight,
His house is a hole of rotting bones,
And in the morn he loudly groans.
He sucks on a bone with meat on the ends,
And lies on a floor with a body that bends,
He has white fangs that have blood, bright red,
And has dark black fur that gets grey round his head.
When children go in there is silence, then screams,
They all run out followed by the thing that has eyes which beam.
His nose is soggy and wet with gunge,
If he sees live meat into it his teeth do plunge.
When the sun sets, deep asleep he will go,
No groans are heard, so the children know,
That the thing within the gloomy hole
Is asleep, fast asleep with those haunted souls.

Larne Barlow (10)
Bursley CP School

THE FOOTBALL FIELD

I like to play on the football pitch
But when it's cold,
You twitch and twitch.
Your strip makes you itch and itch,
When you play on the football pitch.

I like to score in the football game,
And when you score they,
Shout your name.
Your heartbeat doesn't stay the same,
When you play in the football game.

Michael Smith (11)
Bursley CP School

A NEW STEPPING STONE

What's going to happen to me?
I'm being yanked over a hurdle,
It's hurdle 2000 for me,
Laying down a new stepping stone,
A new stepping stone for me.

The horse has got a new jump,
A new fresh jump,
He's trying it for the first time,
The last time maybe,
No matter what happens to him,
It's a new stepping stone for me.

The old oak is distributing its last acorns,
Planting down a new tree,
No matter what happens to them,
It's a new stepping stone for me.

The dogs have had a new kennel,
All fresh clean and new,
No matter what happens to them,
It's a new stepping stone for me.

Richard Hemmings (9)
Church Eaton Endowed (A) Primary School

ANGER

Frowning angrily, scowling terribly,
Smouldering with anger,
'Don't point the finger at me,
Leave me alone and let me be.'
When I'm cross I'm the boss,
My volcano will erupt and spread its angry lava.

The words won't come out, they're stuck in my throat,
'Don't you say anything to rock the boat.'
I get all frantic and shake like a leaf,
My knees start to tremble, all I feel is grief.
'I need a break, so go away,
All I want is my ball back,'
'Okay!'

Faye Wrotchford (10)
Church Eaton Endowed (A) Primary School

YOU BULLY

People stare at me as I go to my new school
At break time they push me and shove me,
My mind says do something about it,
But I can't,
Help! Help!
I'm too scared to tell someone, even Child Line,
They have given me a black eye
Why, why do you do this?
I've heard of people who end up in hospital
Couldn't someone be my friend?
Please help.
There is this other new child
Who has no friends,
And so I ask him
But I went in quickly in case I got bullied.
Now we're great friends,
And I told my teacher and my parents,
I'm not bullied anymore.
So don't put up with
                    Bullying.

Sally-Anne Ashby (9)
Church Eaton Endowed (A) Primary School

SPACE POEM

One day on Earth,
Stacie gave birth,
To a little young astronaut.
His nose was so big,
And his head was so small.

When he grew up he flew a spacecraft,
He flew all the way to Mars.
He refuelled the engine, got in his seat,
And sped off to Pluto.
As he landed a terrible thought struck him,
What if I hit a rock?
That would be the end of him.

He landed with a crash,
It gave his head a bash,
And he died at that moment.
A few aliens had seen the crash,
They decided to bury him quick,
They put up a gravestone,
And they called him St Nick.
But back on Earth Stacie gave birth
To a little young astronaut.

Katie Frost (9)
Church Eaton Primary School

WIND!

Wind whistling calmly,
Softly in the breeze,
Swirling among the trees.
The wind is whistling through my ear
Drifting away all my fear.
Curiously sweeping through the grass
Whooshing past.

Spinning away,
Night and day.
Weakly creeping around,
Making no sound.
The wind's drifting away
With no time to stay.
Softly in the breeze
Swirling among the trees.

Rebekah Herbert (10)
Church Eaton Endowed (A) Primary School

STORMY WEATHER

A calm wind starts to form,
A little kid walks about,
As the stormy weather rushes by,
The wind gets stronger and knocks things over,
It storms round dark corners,
Nothing can stop it,
It hits everything in its path.

The wind whistles in the windows,
All the leaves do a dance,
Lightning splits the sky,
The kid runs for cover under an old apple tree,
Lightning strikes again on the tree,
The wind sweeps up the leaves,
The wind killing the sights.

The kid runs for home,
The wind begins to settle,
The lightning stops,
The leaves stop dancing,
The wind stops from creeping.

Andrew Woodward (10)
Church Eaton Primary School

ENJOY IT

If you have a problem, then forget it!
If you're handicapped or disabled, don't worry!
It ain't no problem, so have fun.
Come on, it's nearly the Millennium,
Make your party plans!
So don't be sad, be happy.
Don't be down and think small,
You're bound to have a good time.

So if you're down and still not happy
Talk to someone, get it sorted.
'Cause you can't get left out,
It's not fair!
Celebrate the year 2000,
Because it's never going to come again,
Enjoy it while you can!
Dance the night away
Don't let anyone tell you different.
If they party
Why shouldn't you!
So put some music on,
Maybe Robbie Williams will do . . . Millennium!

Frances Gibson (9)
Church Eaton Primary School

MY NEIGHBOUR'S DOG

My neighbour's dog is quite fond,
Of jumping in our big blue pond.
He chases twigs,
And guinea pigs.
He jumps around,
Like a hound,
But when he's bored
He sleeps like a lord.

It's got to be my neighbour's dog,
That's soaking all my pansies.
He made my mum furious,
'Cos he jumped up at the laundry,
That's the life of my neighbour's
Bouncy, crazy, soaking dog.

Richard Harper (10)
Church Eaton Endowed (A) Primary School

DOGS

Alsatians,
Dalmatians,
Come in black and white,
Playful and strong,
My dog can write.

Collies,
Like red lollies
They are fun to be with.
They can be bright orange.
My dog's fun to be with.

Puppies
Come in all shapes and sizes.
Big and small,
Fat and thin.
My dog's really small.

Dogs, dogs,
I love dogs.
They're my favourite pet.
I think they're cute and cuddly.
I really love my dog.

Roxanne Hill (9)
Church Eaton Primary School

My Pets

My pets are funny,
All my cats collect mice,
But they never decide to eat them,
We always wonder why,
Why do mice never get eaten?

The cats run through the door,
Waiting for the food,
At night they hunt somewhere,
But I don't know where,
The cats are waiting for food.

My pet fish,
Swims round and round,
A tree stands in the middle,
They keep trying to jump out,
Why do they try to jump out?

My pet dog,
I take him for a walk,
But instead, I don't
He takes me for a walk,
He runs round my feet.

But now I dream of my next pet,
A hamster with the name 'Hamlet,'
He'll sleep all day,
And play all night.

Rachel Massie (9)
Chruch Eaton Primary School

BULLYING

They picked on me!
Laughed at me,
What about world peace,
What about that,
They ain't anything at all like that.

I didn't dare tell anyone
Not even my mum!
No I must keep it to myself,
Like Mum said,
'Don't think about yourself.'

The next day was worse,
And I mean worse!
They came to me, picked on me,
Worse than the usual stuff,
They hit my lip,
When I got in I said I'd fallen over,
Yeah right,
When I got home I said
'Leave me alone.'

Now I feel better after I've told
My mum,
She had a word with the Head,
I knew the children were dead,
I think I've done the right thing,
Well don't you too!

Charlotte Brown (9)
Church Eaton Primary School

FEELINGS

I was unhappy,
As unhappy as could be.
I pushed the door,
Mother yelled don't do that anymore.
I shouted with anger as loud as I could,
I clenched my fists since I thought I should.
Mother was in a mood,
That was definite, no food.

I sat on my head, red whirled through my head,
My thoughts were rushing
And gushing all around me,
Whatever is the matter with me,
Whatever can it be?
It is everything,
Even my favourite thing,
Swimming!

Calm down,
Calm down, I kept saying to myself.
I got up off my bed,
My legs were half dead,
My knees shook,
I took a look,
The sun shone, silence, now the anger has gone.

Katy James (11)
Church Eaton Primary School

WHAT WILL WE DO IN THE YEAR 2000?

What will we do in the year 2000?
Will we be going mad?
Will we go on holiday?
Will you see the year 2000?
Will England win Euro?

Will the Dome be a great hit?
Will you be watching TV all day?
Will something tragic happen?
Will teachers become robots?
Will you party all day?

I know what I'm doing,
Oh yes I do,
Something you won't do,
You promise you won't tell?
No it's a secret.

Will you do something zany?
Will you try your hand at relaxing?
I know it's on my list,
Well whatever you do,
Make it original.

Thomas Beech (10)
Church Eaton Primary School

MY DOG GYP

When I feed Gyp she jumps up and down like a bouncy ball,
She jumps really high and over our wall,
Our friendship is something nothing will break,
I would do anything for her, even jump in a lake.

I play with Gyp in my back garden,
And watch her like my own child and I'm her guardian,
I have to clean up all she does,
I'm not allowed to take her on the bus.

I love her lots and lots,
And she loves to rummage through plant pots,
I love to play fetch with my dog,
We normally play it with a log.

She sleeps in a box,
She's been chased by a fox,
But then she turns wild,
And then turns mild.

Laura James (10)
Doxey Primary School

DINOSAURS

The Velociraptor is fierce and fast,
Just like a cheetah running past,
The Diplodocus is large and slow,
Just like a tortoise lying low,
The T-Rex is enormous and strong,
Like a lion of the jungle.
The Allosaurus has teeth like razor sharp daggers.

David Arkinstall (10)
Doxey Primary School

THE WRATH OF NAN

This morning Mum announced
I've good news to say
Your father and I
Are to go away.

You and your brother
Are to stay with your nan.
We hope to come back
With a deep brown tan.

We arrived early Saturday
Begging to leave,
The nerve of Mum
We just couldn't believe.

Remember last month
The torture, the pain,
Nan screamed and moaned
Just over a stain.

Nan the next day
Began screaming you rat,
All I am asking is
Just straighten the mat.

The wrath of Nan
Began to kick in
When she told me to empty
The rubbish bin.

Natalie Williams (10)
Doxey Primary School

THE RABBIT

I was sitting there,
On a normal day,
Looking at the sky,
And eating hay.

Suddenly I heard,
A noise from above,
I looked up and
I heard a dove.

All at once,
I sensed danger,
And it was a fox,
Who killed the ranger.

The fox said,
Politely to me,
You're going to be,
My lovely tea.

I started to run,
Faster and faster,
But the fox got,
Caught by the master.

Sharon Johnson (11)
Doxey Primary School

CASEY

I have a white and grey cat,
Casey is his name,
He chases mice and butterflies,
And thinks it's a wonderful game.

Casey walks like a floating white balloon,
He licks my dish clear,
On the TV he watches baboons,
When he watches them he gets really near.

Laura Whiting (10)
Doxey Primary School

MY SCHOOL

My school is really cool,
We go swimming on Mondays,
Heartbeat in the week,
We have the nicest teacher you'll ever meet.

The best day for dinners is Monday,
Wednesday and Friday,
We have their lovely chips and other
things lovely too.

At break time we have footballs,
skipping ropes too,
I go in my little corner and play football
with all my mates.

When we go in after break,
We change our library books,
Have a laugh,
Read and talk.

And at the end of the day,
I think I've done really well.
I got a house point maybe,
More or less but now it's time to say,
Goodbye!

Chelsea Pettigrew (10)
Doxey Primary School

COLOURS

Blue is like a cloudy sky
ready to pour with rain.
It goes into the ocean
again and again.

Red is like a shining ruby
crystal clear,
it sparkles brightly.

Yellow is like the enormous sun
always giving light,
you can't look at it
because it is so bright.

Jodie Ashington (10)
Doxey Primary School

SNOW

Snow is falling,
Animals are cold,
Wrap up warm,
The children are told.

The rooftops are covered,
With freezing snow,
The whistling of the wind,
Makes the trees blow.

The hills and mountains,
Are as white as paper,
The streams and lakes,
Turn white later.

Anthony Knapp (10)
Doxey Primary School

NIGHT-TIME ANIMALS

Night-time is a very special time,
The animals all come out in a line,
The owl with its cold hard stare
Flies in the night sky.

The fox running across the dew wet grass,
Looking for its breakfast,
Of rabbits, deer and birds.

The bat with its very sensitive sonar,
Flies through the early morning sky,
Tracking his prey from way up on high.

The deer with antlers as high as can be,
It runs from the fox as quick as lightning,
Then returned home.

Daniel Padley (10)
Doxey Primary School

MY HAMSTER

My hamster's name is Lucy,
She looks like a fluffy ball,
Her eyes are like black marbles staring at the door.

Her claws are like a pointed pair of scissors,
Her teeth are as sharp as a knife,
Her ears are as soft as a fluffy pillow,
And her fur is like a rug on the dusty floor.

Claire Whitehouse (11)
Doxey Primary School

AN ENORMOUS CAT

I saw an enormous cat,
Just like a fierce lion,
Out came his long claws,
Like the blades of chopping scissors.

I saw him at the fish shop,
Scratching on the door,
Wagging his tail as fast
As a sword.

I threw him a scaly fish,
Then he ate it,
He licked his mouth,
I threw him another,
He ate it quicker than the other.

Then I started to walk home,
Then he started to follow me,
I started to run,
As fast as I could,
But he caught up with me.

He turned into a house,
He purred on the door,
Someone answered and said,
'Come in,'
So I just went home.

Christine Gault (10)
Doxey Primary School

THE BLACK CAT

There was a black cat,
He was as black as the blackboard.
And his paws were as white as chalk,
He was the nicest cat I ever knew.

There was a black cat,
As black as could be.
I like black cats,
I like black cats that don't scratch.

The best black cat is my black cat,
He sits on the wall all day,
Like a blackboard he is the funniest of them all.

Michael Webber (10)
Doxey Primary School

ROCKET MAN

Rocket man, rocket man,
He went up to the moon.
He saw a balloon,
It floated up to the moon.
When he saw the balloon,
He saw it go boom.

Rocket man, rocket man,
He saw a ball,
He said 'Oh no,'
It could go so,
But it couldn't say no,
Because it's not alive,
But it went clang and then boom.

Nathan Butlin (9)
Doxey Primary School

MY CAT SUSIE

My cat Susie,
Is awfully choosy.
I give her a fish,
On a round white dish.
She turns her nose up,
She'd rather drink milk from a cup.
She likes to pull,
On a large ball of wool.

Then she goes to find a mouse,
Crawling around the house.
But she has no luck,
So she did some muck,
On the kitchen floor,
Right next to the back door.
Then she goes to sleep at night,
That is her delight.

Janine Davies (10)
Doxey Primary School

THE WORLD

The grass is green,
And the flowers are clean,
The flowers have started to grow,
And the grass has started to glow,
The rainbow is here,
So come and have a look at it.

Melissa Pople (10)
Doxey Primary School

DINNER TIME

'It's dinner time'
Says the teacher.
'Sit up straight
Else you will be late.'

'Line up by the board,'
Through the door we go.
There goes the bell
As I say 'Oh no!'

Dinner was sick,
I didn't even like it.
'Are you OK?' said the lady,
No what's in this.

She said 'Go on to your pudding,'
'But that's a waste' I said,
'Just do it' she said,
'Have a taste.'

I think I will have sandwiches with jam,
Not horrible dinners,
And I'll sit by Sam.

Tomorrow will come,
To set me free,
I'll be sandwiches,
Sitting by Sam and Vicky.

Simmone Williams (9)
Doxey Primary School

AT THE ORPHANAGE

At the orphanage,
There I sat,
At the orphanage,
With my little rat.

At the orphanage,
People run around,
At the orphanage,
They all fall on the ground.

At the orphanage,
There's such a hard bed,
At the orphanage,
That's where I lay my head.

At the orphanage,
I read my book,
At the orphanage,
'It's dinner time' said the cook.

At the orphanage,
With my teddy bear,
At the orphanage,
I heard a noise and said 'Who's there?'

At the orphanage,
It's scary at night,
At the orphanage,
It's not a nice sight.

At the orphanage,
Short people stand,
At the orphanage,
We wave our hands.

And that's what it's like,
At the orphanage.

Vicky Pattyson (9)
Doxey Primary School

SCHOOL DINNERS

Ding, ding the alarm sings
That must mean that dinners in.
Hot dog's and chips, spaghetti of course,
My friend had half a leg of horse.

Time to pick my pudding now
I wonder what I'll have,
I think I'll have cream and jelly both with strawberry jam.

I wander off to my table to eat my gorgeous dinner.
I've just had the best dinner of my life
And I have to go away.
I wonder what I'll have tomorrow,
On a nice clean tray.

Ding, ding the alarm sings
That must mean dinners in.
'Sit down Jim, sit up Vicky' said the dinner lady,
The queue is just about to begin.

Lauren Maple (9)
Doxey Primary School

THE MILLENNIUM

The millennium is a time to cheer,
When men get drunk from too much beer!
The Millennium Dome has just been built,
And Scotsmen men are dancing in a kilt!

People will celebrate for many days,
Which will be done in many ways,
There will be fireworks throughout the night,
The sky around will glow with light.

Claire Gaisford (10)
Doxey Primary School

MY AUNT

My aunt is very old,
She's a hundred and seventy two.
She's always got a cold,
She's far off being new.
My aunt wears very old clothes,
She's got on far too much make up.
She buys dark brown loaves,
She has a special cup for when she has her tea.
When she wants tea she will always ask me!
I want to throw her in the pig sty
Or send her up to the sky!

Caroline Moore (10)
Doxey Primary School

TONIGHT AT NOON

Tonight at noon
Cars will ride us,
Dogs miaow, cats bark,
Lights will make darkness,
Books will read us,
Crocodiles will learn to be reporters,
Cats eat bird food,
Letters will write us,
Doors will open us,
Compasses will draw straight lines,
We will sting bees,
Chairs will sit on us,
Flies will eat frogs,
Plates will eat off us,
People can fly.

Ben Ashwood (10)
Greenacres Primary School

THE OGRES!

As I walk down the street,
I smelt ogres feet.
I carried on walking,
Suddenly I heard talking,
I looked round the hedge,
Sitting on a ledge were two fat ogres,
One was licking his toes, the other was picking his nose,
The ogres looked up and tried to grab my foot,
So I ran and ran but I slipped on some jam,
So did the ogre, he didn't look sober,
I got away at the end of the day,
And never saw an ogre again.

Shane Morris (11)
Greenacres Primary School

TONIGHT AT NOON

Tonight at noon,
There will be a red moon,
Flowers will be stars,
Monkeys drive cars,
Leopards will have stripes,
And babies will smoke pipes,
Bears will miaow
And a teacher will turn into a cow,
Pigs will have all the world power,
The clock will strike a thirteenth hour,
Dogs will wear glasses,
Yesterday will be soon,
Tonight at noon!

Rachael Bonas (11)
Greenacres Primary School

TONIGHT AT THE MILLENNIUM

Cars will hover
Cinemas will be in virtual reality
Games will come to life
Guns will be no more and lasers move in
There will be hotels on the moon
Lightsabres will be real
Computers will have conversations with us
Aliens will live among us
Robots will work for us
Star Trek will be real.

Ben Diamond (10)
Greenacres Primary School

THE TRAIN TO LIVERPOOL

In the station,
Standing about,
Waiting for the train to come around,
Getting so bored it starts to rain.

My train comes round,
I jump straight in,
I tried to find a drinks machine,
But then I find a real big treat.

The treat I find,
Is a real big sweet,
I find my seat,
And fall asleep.

I wake up with a nasty shock,
As the train comes to a halt,
I hear a man shout
'Liverpool's here.'

And then I go outside to hear
My name shouted out,
'Go to the Liverpool ground,
To collect your ticket.'

I go to the Liverpool ground,
Collect my ticket and find my seat,
I watch Liverpool play,
They win five nil, I shout hooray, hooray and celebrate.

Karen Dhaliwal (10)
Greenacres Primary School

TONIGHT AT NOON

Tonight at noon
Doors will sneeze
Eyes will hear
In maths we'll learn English

Pens will talk to us
Food will eat us
Aliens will live on Earth
Footballs will kick us
In PE we will learn science
The Titanic will rise from the sea bed
Books will read us
Cars will have legs
Cats will bark
Ovens will cook us
Crayons will colour us
Televisions will watch us
Radios will listen to us
Martians will play football
Crocodiles will learn to read
Tonight at noon.

Matthew Wedge (10)
Greenacres Primary School

TONIGHT AT NOON

Tonight at noon,
Clocks will tock tick
Bears will eat raw eggs
Computers will be free.

Tonight at noon,
Pigs will fly
And birds won't
Dinosaurs will come back to life.

Tonight at noon,
Cars will fly
Grass will be purple
Flowers will be gold.

Tonight at noon,
Pupils will teach teachers
People will keep tigers as pets
Animals will wear clothes.

James Brown (11)
Greenacres Primary School

TONIGHT AT NOON

Tonight at noon,
The moon will jump over the cow,
Astronauts will fly to the Earth,
Frogs will eat anacondas,
Food will eat humans,
Worms will eat blackbirds,
Birds will kill cats,
Chairs will walk,
Houses will make people,
Martians will live on Earth,
PC's will play us,
Dogs will talk,
Humans will bark,
Toys will play us,
Thieves will catch police,
Dirt bikes will ride us,
Nuts will crack us,
Books will grow legs,
Tonight at noon.

Chris Chapman (10)
Greenacres Primary School

HOLIDAY

Driving down the motorway
Looking forward to our holiday
Singing with excitement and glee
Wondering how our holiday will be.

When we finally arrive
After a very long drive
We see our caravan in a park close by
Close to the beach, I'm full of joy.

In the park I go walking
Listening to different people talking
Watching small children playing
Wondering together what they are saying.

I wonder what the child's kite can see
So high above the world and me
And if the birds are friends to him
As I am friends with Jack and Jim.

Kirsty Burford (10)
Greenacres Primary School

MISSING POEM

I miss the way my cat Sooty used to come up to me and sit on me,
I miss the way he played with me,
I miss his soft furry coat and his bright yellow eyes.

I miss his meow in the morning and I miss not feeding him,
I miss him sleeping on my bed in the morning,
I miss the way he ate his food,
The thing I miss most is his sweet little face.

Lucy Coles (10)
Greenacres Primary School

BUBBLES

I miss my hamster, Bubbles,
I miss her soft fur,
I miss her playing on her wheel,
I miss her twitchy nose.

I miss the way she cleans herself,
I think it's very sweet,
I miss her when she sits on my hand,
But I don't miss when she bites me.

I miss the way she runs in her ball all around the floor,
I miss the way she looks at me,
With her sweet little face,
But most of all I miss my best friend, Bubbles.

Caroline Prince (10)
Greenacres Primary School

MY DOG

My dog is the dawn of my day,
He jumps on my bed and licks me in welcome.
If I'm sad he's always there for me,
I wonder if he will meet another dog one day and what would it be?

Would it be as nice as mine can be?
Or would it just be mean?
He might stay the way he is as loving as can be,
It's not only my love for him,
It's the sparkling in his eyes
And the lovely ginger fur on his back with white below,
But most of all I know he loves me.

Clint Wilson (10)
Greenacres Primary School

A TRAIN TO THE MOON

Into the station,
Standing around,
Waiting for the train,
That comes around.

It's rustle and bustle to find a seat,
It's going to be a long trip.
I sit down to eat,
I give the butler a tip.

I look out the window,
See all the planets that we pass,
There's a quick show,
With an actress called Julia Cass.

I fall asleep,
I hear a bang so I wake up,
I look out the window, see some aliens,
I look up.

See the time,
It's one o'clock, the train stops,
I jump right off,
I walk around the space mall.

Hours went past,
It's 4 o'clock, I had a space burger,
Then I went to the station,
Saw some green Martians.

Went to the train, found a seat
And sat down, off to earth we go.

Aimee Edwards (11)
Greenacres Primary School

WHEN I GROW UP

When I grow up
I think I'd like to
Be a chef, because
I love to cook
And I do a bit myself.

I'll be like Ainsley Harriot
With a bit of Percy Pepper,
And Suzy Salt,
While fun is on the way.

I'll own a humungous
Restaurant with a large
Kitchen and a dinning room
Just like the Titanic's,
There will be a dance floor.

And the restaurant will
Be named after me,
I can see it now!
Beth's Restaurant.

Why I'll be the head chef,
There'll be an orchestra
Playing music in the
Queen's honour and that's
When I grow up.

Bethany Wroe (11)
Greenacres Primary School

CANDY

I miss my dog, Candy.
I miss the way she looked at me
With her amber, glowing eyes
I miss the way she'd play with me
All day long.

I miss taking her for a walk
And to see her running across the fields
She'd race back to me, tail wagging
Happy to run free.

I miss her warm body lying across my feet
Warm and cosy snuggled up to me
Her silky, brown fur, soft and smooth.
How I miss Candy, my best friend.

Claire Whithouse (11)
Greenacres Primary School

I MISS MY DOG

I miss my dog
Because she got put down
When she had eight puppies
We had to give the puppies away
My nan had one
But it wrecked her house
I'm feeling very sad
Because Tasha has gone
She was a good dog.

Joe Grimley (11)
Greenacres Primary School

FIVE FANTASTIC CHILDREN

Five fantastic children
Stroking a tiger's paw
Lewis got his head bit off
Then there were four.

Four fantastic children
Watching a swinging monkey
Chris fell off the wall
Then there were three.

Three fantastic children
Playing at the zoo
Peter fell in the cage
Then there were two.

Two fantastic children
Feeding the swans
Nick tripped over
Then there was one.

One fantastic child
On his way home
Tripped and fell
Then there was none.

Ashley Gough (10)
Greenacres Primary School

WEIRD FRIENDS

I have two very important friends
One named Rachael and the other Aimee
I'm glad I met them
In my new school
But the greatest friend of all is Kirsty
She is quiet but is fun
You will never guess the funniest thing she's done
Someone put wine in her hamburger
She ate it of course
And then had a hangover!
But my extraordinary friend is
Miss Gossip Queen 1999
Karen who gossips the day away
With a chat here and there
They are my weird friends.

Lucy Shutt (11)
Greenacres Primary School

SPAIN

When I went to Spain
My mum kept saying it would rain.
It took four hours to get there,
But I don't really care.

I love jumping in the pool
Because it is nice and cool.
When I went to Sunny Bay,
Everyone kept saying Olé.

Carl Baldwin (9)
Longwood County Primary School

RUNNING

Trainers on,
Hands tremble,
Hair sways,
Feet move.

Wind blows,
Face dribbles,
Wind whistles,
Feet bounce.

Feet still,
Feel good,
Trainers off,
Go to sleep.

Jodie Withers (9)
Longwood County Primary School

RUNNING

Trainers skid,
Heart pounds,
Hands shake,
Arms sway.

Mouth blows,
Hair flows,
Feet slide,
Legs stride.

Feel wonderful,
Happy,
Look at countryside.

Luke Slater (8)
Longwood County Primary School

RUNNING

Shoes on,
Heart thumps,
Winds whistle,
Hair swirls,
Go!
Feet bounce,
Running fast,
Lightning flash,
Thunder crash,
Go!
Feel happy,
Out of breath,
Slow down,
Listen to Mum
Shout . . .
'Dinner!'

Katie Tallis (9)
Longwood County Primary School

MY JOURNEY TO DISNEYLAND

Dazzling sea down below,
Loads of people saying hello,
Singing birds all up above,
But then guess what I saw,
All the birds flying high,
Up into the morning sky,
The sun shines down on top of me,
I really wanted to jump into the sea.

Leanne Orton (9)
Longwood County Primary School

A JOURNEY TO AMERICA

When I went to America
it was good fun
it took four hours to get there
it was fun, fun, fun.

When I went to America
I went on an aeroplane
I said 'Wow this is
fun, fun, fun.'

When I went to America
I went to an American school
it had good things there
they were fun, fun, fun.

Elizabeth Emery (9)
Longwood County Primary School

SURFING

Deep breaths,
Feet place,
Eyes closed,
Out to sea.

Big wave,
Swept out,
Jump up,
Catapulted off.

Open eyes,
Troubles gone,
Just feel,
Sea song.

Olivia Shepherd (8)
Longwood County Primary School

AFRICAN ANIMALS

Nelly the elephant with the bony knees,
Please come out and play with the bees,
They like honey you like hay,
Come outside and we can play.

Gurty the roo, away she flew,
With a hop and a skip and a toodaloo,
She went to the park and played on the slides,
She laughed and giggled and split her sides.

Charlie the cheetah,
He would always beat ya in a game or race,
He would use black magic or win on luck,
And hide his cheeky face.

Danielle Worrell (10)
Longwood County Primary School

WINTER DAYS

Winter is here, winter is here,
Snow covers the land in white silk.
Birds cry to the cruel coldness,
Nature dying as the days get colder.

Winter is here, winter is here,
Misty clouds cover the happy skies.
Jack Frost leaping around leaving a trail,
Fires on, chimneys smoking.

Winter is here, winter is here,
Nights drawing in.
Days with less light,
Wind rustling all around.

Sinead Langford (11)
Longwood County Primary School

WINTER!

Through the winter days
I travel through the crispy snow.
Winds rattle at all the doors even the leafless trees.

The silver mirror on the ground
Shows the moon up above.
Watery phases on the floor,
Look at the feathers coming down.

Winter is here from Jack Frost
Who steals the warmth from the air.
He's left cold in the sky,
Sparkling seas and icy waters.

Winter, winter, here again
Rosy cheeks, reddish noses.
Fear in autumn as it loses its
Shining days.

Kielea Woods (11)
Longwood County Primary School

THE CAT-EATING CAT

The cat-eating cat
Is always fat
He's blamed for each and every death
He drags away his prey
He leaves the bones in other homes
And always gets away.

Shaun Cordell (10)
Longwood County Primary School

MY RUSH TO HOLIDAY

One day we're going away
I get up very early in the morning
And I rush to my clothes to pack my suitcase
I rush to eat my breakfast
I rush to clean my teeth
I rush to clean my face
I rush, rush, rush
I rush to get in the car
I rush to my dad to start the car
I rush to get out of the drive
I rush, rush, rush
I rush my dad to get out the traffic
I rush my dad to get there
I rush, rush, rush
I rush my dad to find the caravan
And when we get there I rush myself to calm down.

Katie Stanley (10)
Longwood County Primary School

I'M ONLY 11

Oh man, I feel so weak,
We're decomposing as we speak.
We're all about to die,
Then we will float up to the sky.
I don't want to go to heaven,
For Pete's sake I'm only 11.

Victoria Dubberley (10)
Longwood County Primary School

WINTER

W hite snowflakes fall
I cicles hang high
N ippy winds blow
T here is white everywhere
E veryone wants sun
R oads with crispy snow
   Winter is really cold.

Lisa Tooley (9)
Longwood County Primary School

VINDALOO

Spicy hot, fiery hot, going down my throat.
It's hot, I love it a lot, *gulp.*
Spicy hot, fiery hot, going down my throat,
Eugh - it's too hot! Quick, water - come to me.
Ssssss, Aaaarrr
Spicy hot, fiery hot, going down my throat.
Slobber, slobber, chomp, chomp, gulp, gulp, gulp.
Mum! Can I have some more?
Slobber, chomp, gulp, gulp. She gave me some more.
Slobber, chomp, gulp, gulp. But the steam came up like fire.
Slobber, chomp, gulp, gulp. I ate some curry.
Poof! Poof! Steam came out my ears.
Mum! Naan bread please.
Slobber, chomp, gulp, gulp. I picked up the naan bread.
Slobber, chomp, gulp, gulp and dunked it in my rice and curry.
Oh slobber, chomp, gulp, gulp, curry fills my tummy!

Sarah Kent (9)
Needwood CE (A) Primary School

CAST A SPELL

I'll start with the nose of a dog,
   then the tusk of a hog,
      and bird's wing,
         bee's sting,
            tongue of snake,
               garden rake.

Roast and rubble, let's make trouble.

Eye of rat,
   ear of cat,
      a wing of a bat,
         dust off the mat,
            now put in a fat hat
               with a cow pat.

Roast and rubble, let's make trouble.

Now let's put a rattle of an adder,
That'll make everyone sadder.

Roast and rubble, now we've made trouble bubble.

Catherine Walker (10)
Needwood CE (A) Primary School

THE SPELL'S BEEN CAST

With this potion people will die . . .
Let's drop in a cat's eye.
Now let's put in a bee's sting
Next we'll put a bird's wing.

> Fire bubbles blow!
> Cauldron bubbles go!
> Bubble, bubble,
> Fire burns trouble,
> Trouble, trouble,
> Cat's eye bubble.

What about a leg of frog?
A wing of bat? An ear of dog?
A tail of skunk? Shell of snail?
Liver of a rat? Or a fin of a whale?

> Fire bubbles blow!
> Cauldron bubbles go!
> Bubble, bubble,
> Fire burns trouble,
> Trouble, trouble,
> Cat's eye bubble.

Jodie Baxter (11)
Needwood CE (A) Primary School

CAST A SPELL

A dash of this, a dash of that,
A wing of a rotten bat.
A cat's tongue, a rat's tail,
A human being's fingernail.
Some frogs' legs, some snails' shells,
Some smelly water from the water wells.

Steaming, steaming in the pot,
Keep my potion rotten and hot.

Ear wax upon an axe,
Some slimy goo aglow,
Some frogspawn, clothes worn
By anyone you know.

Steaming, steaming in the pot,
Keep my potion rotten and hot.

Rebecca Roberts (10)
Needwood CE (A) Primary School

OH RAIN

Oh rain, oh rain, a drizzle or a downpour,
Whatever you are, you cause a puddle.
Oh rain, oh rain, you cause so much chaos.
Oh rain, oh rain, you teem you pour, you shower.
Oh rain, oh rain, you say to me, 'Tip a tap tap.'
Oh rain, oh rain, the way your pour, I love.
Oh rain, oh rain, the way I get wet, I adore.
Oh rain, oh rain, 'Tipper tapper tip.'
Oh rain, oh rain, 'Tip tap flick.'
Oh rain, oh rain,
You're lovely.

Sam Murphy (10)
Needwood CE (A) Primary School

THE WRESTLE

I quarrelled with my sister,
I hit her on the bum,
She called me a pig,
And I called her dumb.

I quarrelled with my sister,
She threw a shoe at me,
I jumped on her back,
And bit her one, two, three.

I quarrelled with my sister,
She shouted a lot more,
I started to snigger,
When she fell onto the floor.

I quarrelled with my sister,
She wailed out loud for Mum,
She came running with her friend,
Who owned a huge shotgun.

I quarrelled with my sister,
They yelled at us a lot,
By the end of the long lecture,
We really felt like clots.

Emma Preston (9)
Needwood CE (A) Primary School

BACON, BACON

Bacon, bacon
juicy and crisp.
It's all in my tummy
a wonderful dish.

Bacon, bacon
chewy and soft.
Oh I could never
take all the fat off.

Bacon, bacon
just so greasy.
May I have some more?
Pleasey, pleasey.

Bacon, bacon
all so crackly.
Can I have some more?
Thanky, thanky.

Bacon, bacon
sour and salty.
Smells like hot
chicken balti.

Guy Atkinson (9)
Needwood CE (A) Primary School

MINT CHOC CHIP ICE-CREAM

Mint choc chip ice-cream,
I love you *so* much,
You're sweet to eat
And soft to touch.
Oh yes, ice-cream,
I love you very much.

Mint choc chip ice-cream,
You creamy, minty stuff,
You're *so* sloshy,
I think you're divine
And very fluffy
Oh yes, ice-cream,
I love you very much.

Mint choc chip ice-cream,
You remind me of parties
And chocolate and holidays.
I love all those little brown chips
And the cold ice-cream.
Mmmmm
Oh yes, ice-cream,
I love you very much.

Amy Bendall (10)
Needwood CE (A) Primary School

CAST A SPELL

Triple trouble, boil, bubble,
Around the cauldron, let's stir up trouble.

Bat's wing,
Bee's sting,
Snake's fork,
Rotten pork.

Triple trouble, boil, bubble,
Around the cauldron, let's stir up trouble.

A cow's tail,
A wolf's wail
Tongue of dog
Toe of frog.

Triple trouble, boil, bubble,
Around the cauldron, let's stir up trouble.

Megan Atkinson (11)
Needwood CE (A) Primary School

SUMMER BREEZE

Pansies, poppies, dandelions, daffodils,
All sway in the wind,
What a sight it was to see,
They were swaying together
In the same field,
But when the wind stopped
It was calm and the flowers
In different positions.

Natasha Broadhurst (9)
Newton Regis Primary School

TEACHER'S PETS

'Teacher, Teacher, there's a lion in the toilet.'
'No it's not, it's my pet lion, Leo.'

'Teacher, Teacher, there's a monkey in the dining hall.'
'No it's not, it's my pet monkey, Monty.'

'Teacher, Teacher, there's a snake in the playground.'
'No it's not, it's my pet snake, Sammy.'

'Teacher, Teacher, there's a meerkat in the kitchen.'
'No it's not, it's my pet meerkat, Mike.'

'Teacher, Teacher, there's an alligator in the gym.'
'No it's not, it's my pet alligator, Alex.'

'Teacher, Teacher, there's a zebra in the library.'
'No it's not, it's my pet zebra, Zoe.'

'Teacher, Teacher, there's a parrot in the staff room.'
'No it's not, it's my pet parrot, Polly.'

'Teacher, Teacher, there's a dinosaur in the class room.'
'*Run!*'

Tom Martin (9)
Newton Regis Primary School

MY CHEERFUL SONG

If you want a cheerful song,
To help you go along,
It will cheer you up,
And it might be good luck,
So pick a cheerful song.

Terri South (9)
Newton Regis Primary School

FLYING MY KITE

In the park I fly my kite,
and watch it soar into flight.
In the park there's lots of space,
the wind is blowing in my face.

Further and further away it goes,
its tail is trimmed with lots of bows.
Now it's a small speck in the sky,
over the treetops, it's very high.

It's higher than the trees and sun,
I'm really having lots of fun.
But alas, it's half-past three,
I've got to go home for tea.

Clare Louise Jones (9)
Newton Regis Primary School

THE MILLENNIUM BUG

The millennium bug has ten legs, six eyes
and he's very, very big for his own little size.
He's not in the computer, he's not inside the phone,
so if you don't see him, don't worry and don't moan.
He walks along on his own little feet
singing a song and moving to the beat.
So on Jan 1st 2000 when you've cleared your head
celebrate the new century and tumble out of bed.
'Cause if you want to see him, he will come out only at dawn,
to look just at the dewdrops sitting on the lawn.

Rachel Gray (9)
Newton Regis Primary School

THE BIRD

It flies with its silver wings
Singing out loud over valleys like opera
Never knowing when it will find its nest to perch upon
Swaying in the wind, swaying as it sings.

Grace Coverson (9)
Newton Regis Primary School

THE MILLENNIUM PARTY

I'm the Millennium Bug
the tape player takes the tape and gobbles it up,
like the video recorder instead gives it a suck.

The digital clock goes spinning still
till it takes a headache pill.
Our microwave is made of steal
with the turkey on the wheel.
Traffic lights think they're disco lights
spinning all the colours tonight.

The 1990s have been and gone
we're all happy so let's carry on.
Having a party in the street
lots of people we're going to meet
the milkman, the postman, the DJ too,
the window cleaner, the lollipop man,
what are we going to do?

Have a happy time with all your friends,
this is the time the fun never ends.

Hannah Wetton (8)
Oakridge Primary School

THE TECHNICAL PARTY

All electric things get ready to party,
I'm the Millennium Bug,
I'm gonna mess up everything technical,
And walk in like a thug!

Disco lights mean traffic jams,
And really crazy video cams,
Radios provide the sound,
PC discs aren't spinning round.

Your credit cards won't come back,
When the bank machines go obscene,
With luck your money may attack!
And microwaves dancin' with your beans.

You're really gonna like the year 2000
And I promise you *it'll be fun!*
With all my friends,
In the year 2000, don't miss it!
It's just begun!

Matthew Taylor (8)
Oakridge Primary School

THE MILLENNIUM BUG PARTY

I'm the Millennium Bug
I'm going to be here
very soon.
You will see me
and I'll see you too.

I'm the Millennium Bug
I do not look like a slug.
Maybe I'll turn your computer off
or maybe you will find you woke up at nine o'clock.

I might turn your heater off.
Take a guess who it might be!
Me of course
but you won't know where I am
because I'll be behind the sauce.

The traffic lights will be changing round
but don't make a big sound.
There will be a lot of dancing
and it will look like a reindeer prancing.

Milly Parkes (7)
Oakridge Primary School

CELEBRATION 2000

The twenty-first century,
will be great so let's celebrate.
With fireworks and lots
of fun; My computer is going
round the bend, all I do
is *spend, spend, spend.*

I've lost all my money
I've drank a bit too much.
My dad can't believe the
flashing traffic lights.

My phone won't stop ringing
I think my head is going
to go *bang.* It's all great.
The football will be
great
so let's celebrate.

Alexander Dodd (9)
Oakridge Primary School

THE TECHNICAL DISCO

I'm the Millennium Bug I will make:
the video recorder take videos and not give them back,
like pass the parcel, but never give.
The digital clocks go spinning
till they take a little headache pill.
Microwaves are made of steel,
with a disco turkey on a wheel.
Traffic lights think they are disco lights
with all different colours tonight.
Computers are my one desire,
I'll make them all go haywire.
Shop tills are making money,
their party is so funny.
1990's have gone,
but let's carry on the fun.
I'm the Millennium Bug,
I'm a technical thug.

Sarah Parkinson (9)
Oakridge Primary School

THE MILLENNIUM BUG

The bug is moving in,
I know what will happen if he is to win,
He might make my Gameboy go mad
And that will be very sad.
The turkey's going round and round,
It's making a very loud sound.
The traffic lights are going mad,
I don't know anything quite so bad.

The clock is going tick-tock,
In Index there is nothing in stock.
There is nothing to eat,
Just buy me a treat.
The Millennium Bug is so nice,
It may give you a trip to Venice.

Ryan Nokes (8)
Oakridge Primary School

MAD COW DISEASE FOR COMPUTERS

The Millennium Bug is so kind and gentle
I didn't think it was
supposed to be mental!

The turkeys whizzing round and round.
Money's disappearing by the pound!
Is it really true
It's affected the animals in the zoo?
The ravens have gone raving mad
Even the laughing hyenas are sad!

Traffic lights from green to red
(at least that's what the policeman said)
My violin's playing itself
My carpentry set just made a shelf!

Marks and Spencer's special offer
They've attacked a crazy shopper!
The twentieth century is very big trouble,
Nineteen ninety's burst like a bubble!

The Millennium Bug I'm sorry to say
Has blown my poetry all away.
So . . . I've finished!

Hannah Hulme (9)
Oakridge Primary School

CELEBRATION 2000

It's the Year 2000 time to party,
time to party with all your friends.

This is the year where the fun never ends.
Traffic lights are disco DJ's.
all your friends come over to stay.
Turkeys dance on the microwave wheel,
and in the end it tastes like steel.

Digital clocks have been on the booze,
and after that they have a big, big snooze.
People going to see the Dome,
perhaps it will be a future home.
The video recorder throws out streamers,
maybe they were just futuristic dreamers..

That's 2000 for you,
I promise it won't bore you.

Ceri Waltho (9)
Oakridge Primary School

CELEBRATION 2000

Midnight came
everyone started playing a game.
The music was on,
the drinks were all gone.
Food was on the table
for those who were able.

The computer stopped and had a party.
There's a lot of people in a mardy.
The traffic lights were going crazy
and I had to tell my sister, Maisie.

The hospital machines stopped,
and all the balloons popped.
People tried to have a dance,
they were singing and shouting in advance.
The traffic is going the wrong way.
We have had a silly day.

Emma Waldron (9)
Oakridge Primary School

THE MILLENNIUM BUG

The Millennium Bug is coming in
I know what will happen if he is to win
He will make my computer go mad
But maybe this thing is not so bad
The microwave is going crazy
Like a wild daisy.

The bank keeps on giving me money
And I think it is very funny
The traffic lights think they're disco lights
And you can see them from different sights
The tape machine keeps on throwing out
The tapes inside, all about.

The washing machine is throwing clothes out
Because it thinks they're streamers
My watch is spinning round like mad
I wish he would stop being so bad.

Sophie Barrett (8)
Oakridge Primary School

THE PARTY OF THE CENTURY

Twelve o'clock struck!
Then they start to sing,
so let's all make a big ring.
Traffic lights go crazy,
red, yellow and green
flashing like disco lights
which have gone round the bend.
Even Daisy the cow will not give milk.
Everyone's drunk,
they have drank too much beer.
Everyone stops and starts
to sing on the pier.
Be warned
it is coming to you!

Catherine Le Chevalier (8)
Oakridge Primary School

MILLENNIUM PARTY

Millennium's here, more people appear.
Hospitals going haywire
Even the public phone wire.

Checkouts throwing streams
People acting like screamers
I thought it was going to be gentle
But now it has gone totally mental.

The computer stopped and had a party
And all the people were in a mardy.
The dinner was on the table
For those who were able.
The music was on
And the drinks were all gone.

The millennium party has just begun!

Edward Wallbank (9)
Oakridge Primary School

MILLENNIUM DISCO BUG

The computers will shatter,
To the bug it won't matter,
A crazy clock spins with the dishes,
While Cinderella makes some wishes.

She yells up to her fairy godmother,
'The cooker won't switch on, oh bother!'
The bug is on the winning flash,
Because some cars are going to crash.

All the tapes chucked in the bin,
While CDs move on the biscuit tin,
The turkey's on the chicken's face,
He put the duck in the horse's space.

The bug can't help it, he's a little con,
I hope it changes in the year 2001.

George Wilson (9)
Oakridge Primary School

CELEBRATION 2000

Midnight came,
People dancing around the streets,
Drinking lager and beer,
Drinks were on the table,
For those who were able.
Will the bug really win?

Checkouts in streamers,
Deliveries were all out,
People are hungry,
So they get into lots of fights,
With some frights.
Will the bug really win?

The turkey's twirling around and around,
And the money escaping by the pounds,
Traffic lights from green to red,
The twentieth century is in trouble,
And the nineties just burst like a bubble.
Will the bug really win?

Well this is just a sin,
If you ask me,
Well the Millennium Bug . . .
Has won?

David Bowen (8)
Oakridge Primary School

THE MILLENNIUM BUG

The Millennium Bug is spreading around
Jumping from one object in a bound.
He's made the computer mad
because he's very bad.

The traffic lights have gone crazy
the bank is really lazy.
My tape recorder is dancing,
my electric blanket is prancing.

The traffic lights are flashing
all the cars are crashing.
The televisions have got the fever
and pushing too hard on their levers.

Sophie Knight (8)
Oakridge Primary School

WHITE CAT ON A FROZEN POOL

From an ivory spool,
    The frozen pool,
        With hoar frost laid,
            The white cat's shade,
                Then how it froze,
                    Suspended fish in prose,
                      By the winter glass,
                        Magically passed.

Emma Ralls (8)
Peartree Primary School

COMING TO SCHOOL

No breakfast
  Running fast
    Coaches stopping
      Children coughing
        Cars screeching
          Teachers teaching
            Bell ringing
              Everyone singing.

Austin Lockett (8)
Peartree Primary School

CELEBRATION 2000

The Year 2000 holds lots of sports
from 2 to 18.
It's fun and exciting
so get to a port this very minute.
Catch a train, catch a bus,
catch a ferry, catch a plane
but what's the point of going abroad?
It's held in Great Britain as well!
But don't worry if you miss New Year's Day
it's held throughout the year.

Thomas Henry Lister (10)
St Christopher's RC Primary School, Codsall

YEAR 2000!

Everywhere will be,
zooming busy with housework robots.
Everyone will see
that they do such a lot.
Dusting clocks and cleaning floors,
watching films like Sliding Doors.
Washing up and making beds,
sorting arguments and banging heads.
Cleaning out hamsters' cages,
running around in rages.

Then there probably will be
life-size Beanies that act like Furbys.
(Example life-size Beanies full of beans,
press their tummies and they scream!)
Or maybe they will be the same
always sweet and cuddly.
'Cause I know what Year 2000 means!

Kimberley Everitt (10)
St Christopher's RC Primary School, Codsall

CELEBRATING MILLENNIUM 2000

Celebrating the millennium,
it is very near.
Counting down to 12 o'clock
then we'll all cheer.
All hold hands together and
sing Auld Lang Syne.
The sound of shouting and laughter,
and drinking of champagne and wine.

Kathryn Lampitt (9)
St Christopher's RC Primary School, Codsall

MILLENNIUM THE SECOND

The millennium is a great time . . .
Astronauts living on Mars
it would be cool to live in the stars.
New bugs, all kinds of slugs.
Cars with safety bars.
Pencils that write themselves.
Sharpeners that sharpen themselves.
Oh what a great time.
There could be world peace
And no more military bases,
Or planes.
Not even army tanks.
I never, ever thought it would be so cool.

Alexander Hatfield (9)
St Christopher's RC Primary School, Codsall

MILLENNIUM!

M is for millennium, the time to party.
I   is for Internet, I wonder what's on?
L is for launch of the Millennium Dome.
L is for library, there might be new books.
E is for exclamation mark.
N is for nurse who makes us better.
N is for nature and helping the environment.
I   is for impossible which nothing is.
U is for the Universe which was made by God.
M is for *millennium* which we'll celebrate soon . . .

Amy Eardly (8)
St Christopher's RC Primary School, Codsall

MILLENNIUM

In the millennium anything could happen.
A space hotel built on the moon.
Wart covered aliens taking over our world.
All this could happen so soon.

In the millennium, peace in our time.
No more killing or hate.
An alien may be a better leader
Before it is too late.

In the millennium we could be rich
And I will buy a fast car.
My mum will wear designer clothes
And my family will travel afar.

In the millennium anything could happen.
People could grow their own wings.
St Christopher's may win the Football League
And the world could be full of wonderful things.

James Hayes (8)
St Christopher's RC Primary School, Codsall

THE MILLENNIUM

The millennium is here,
Let's give a big cheer.
We'll all kiss and hug,
And forget the Millennium Bug.

We could all have a party at home,
And then should visit the Millennium Dome.
I think everybody should have good fun
Now the 20th Century is done.

Alexander Mullen-Jones (10)
St Christopher's RC Primary School, Codsall

Millennium, Millennium

Millennium, millennium
who knows what it will bring?
Good things, bad things,
Who knows?

Millennium, millennium,
Some will be happy,
Some will be sad.
We will never know.

The millennium is coming very soon,
Get ready to sing and shout out loud
And do the countdown:
10, 9, 8, 7, 6, 5, 4, 3, 2, 1 - *It's the year 2000!*

Annamaria Casa (10)
St Christopher's RC Primary School, Codsall

New Changes

I wonder whether pigs could fly.
I wonder whether fish have legs.
I wonder what kind of food we will buy.
I wonder whether elephants will hatch out of eggs.

I wonder whether trees are money.
I wonder whether it rains cats and dogs.
I wonder whether the weather is sunny.
I wonder what colours frogs will be.
But to see all these things we must wait
for the Year 2000!

Samantha Taylor (12)
St Christopher's RC Primary School, Codsall

THE MILLENNIUM

The millennium is drawing closer,
A time to celebrate,
A new century,
A wonderful new year.

The computer world has the Millennium Bug,
When the clock strikes 12 the world will all hug.
Will all the programmes have worked
And engineers be on red alert?

Will it be fun with a surprise?
Will it change the rest of our lives?

A time to look forward,
With memories behind,
A super, happy new year to all mankind!

Robyn Hayley Morais (9)
St Christopher's RC Primary School, Codsall

YEAR 2000

Millennium is coming to the world.
Millennium is coming to the world.

Year 2000 will be great.
Year 2000 will be great.

Lots of things to try and test.

The year 2000 will be better,
Than all the other years put together.

Jonathan Maley (9)
St Christopher's RC Primary School, Codsall

WHAT COULD HAPPEN IN THE MILLENNIUM?

What could happen in the millennium?
Could aliens come to Earth from space
or rubbish start to really pollute the place?
What could happen in the millennium?

What could happen in the millennium?
Will peace be ever made?
Then less gravestones would be laid.
What could happen in the millennium?

What could happen in the millennium?
What would happen to every friend
if the world does end?
What could happen in the millennium?

Elizabeth Metcalfe (8)
St Christopher's RC Primary School, Codsall

THE MILLENNIUM IS COMING

M illennium is coming.
I nteresting things are happening.
L ots of new things happening too.
L ike a new Millennium Dome.
E veryone's waiting for the day.
N ever again will we see the years that have gone.
N ow we better get ready for the 21st Century.
I n another 1000 years I wonder what will be happening.
U nderstanding is the key.
M illennium I hope you have lots of exciting things in hand for me.

Roseanne Gee (10)
St Christopher's RC Primary School, Codsall

INVENTION 2000

I wonder what's new in the year 2000.
I wonder what new inventions there will be.
New friends, new computers?
New war inventions?
Helpful inventions, boring inventions, silly inventions?
Girls' inventions, boys' inventions?
New games?
Big inventions, small inventions, medium size inventions?
Inventions for emergency services?
Ideas for inventions?
Typing inventions?
All we need to do is sit down and wait.

Jack O'Donovan (8)
St Christopher's RC Primary School, Codsall

CELEBRATION 2000

It's gonna be big,
It's gonna be huge,
It's gonna be cool.
It's the year 2000.
People will party,
People will dance,
People will be in bed,
But not I.
When the clock strikes midnight we will scream.
Happy New Year!

Jamie Halliwell (10)
St Christopher's RC Primary School, Codsall

WAR IN THE MILLENNIUM

Bombs go down
with a loud sound.

Holes in the ground
appear all around.

Guns never stop
people drop.

Buildings falling down
in the old town.

2000 war is not
safe to be.

The field is dark
by the bomb's mark.

Think who thought
a war was brought.

Joseph Hill (9)
St Christopher's RC Primary School, Codsall

CELEBRATION 2000

Lights flickering,
Wires buzzing,
Birds singing,
People shouting,
Cars *brumming,*
Bang!
Celebration 2000.

Alastair Mason (9)
St Christopher's RC Primary School, Codsall

MILLENNIUM 2000

The survivors of the year 2000.

Millennium 2000 is just like a normal year.
People just have parties for the century.
or street parties.
I wonder what millennium 2000
will be like.
What cars will we drive?
Will we drive spaceships?
We might drive big sports cars
or we might be rich.
We might not be paying bills.
Africa will be happy not sad.
They will have money to help their country.
We will be better, not worse.

Siobhan Fern-Feeney (9)
St Christopher's RC Primary School, Codsall

STREET PARTIES

Street parties.
Let's celebrate
the millennium.
Start it off in the street,
welcome it in.
The start of a new century
plus another thousand years.
The year 2000 is coming our way!

Joanne Ledder (10)
St Christopher's RC Primary School, Codsall

New Inventions In The Year 2000

I can't wait until the year 2000
Because there will be a lot of joy.
New inventions are good to see
And I can't wait for a brand-new toy.

New inventions are good to play
I will play with it every night and day.
I will play with it every night and day
And they will play with it dozens of times.

The new inventions will be a big, big toy,
I will have a lot of joy
Because I will have my big, big toy
And, of course, it will be the year 2000.

William Blacker (9)
St Christopher's RC Primary School, Codsall

The Stars At Night

The stars at night twinkle,
They twinkle with all their might
As the moon shines brighter
They look as though they are fading.
If I could afford a rocket
I would fly around the world
And touch every star in sight.
But if I could fly
I'd fly up to raise money for charity
And build a home in space
Where people could live.

Edward Evans (10)
St Christopher's RC Primary School, Codsall

PARTY TIME TWO

The millennium is almost here
You only have to wait three-quarters of a year.
You can go to the dazzling new Dome
Or have a feast at home.
Delicious, delicious!
Any minute comes a new invention
But the computer bug is getting too much attention.
Brilliant ways of transportation, *wahoo!*
Any time you want to
Brill!
Excellent ways of education.
New ways of calculation.
Lots of places to visit too.
Soon you won't want to go to the zoo
So go on have some fun
Celebrating the millennium.

Omoregie Nehikhare (9)
St Christopher's RC Primary School, Codsall

THE DOME!

The Millennium Dome will come
And may surprise my mum.
There may be pop stars and lots of fun
There may even be a racing run.
There will be new things and brain-bursting stuff
And we might play blind man's bluff.
We think that Jesus will be 2000 years old.
In the Dome, will it be hot, will it be cold?
Will we have new heavy metal bands or maybe rave?
Anyway, anyhow there will be lots of fun.

Thomas Griffin (8)
St Christopher's RC Primary School, Codsall

School In The Millennium

Hip, hip, hooray, it's a new millennium today.
I'm also in Y5 today. Hooray!
What will my teacher be like, strict or calm
Or will she blow up and rattle like an alarm?
I like PE, it is filled with lots of sport
And normally you walk like a horse.
If you want to become a scientist you have to study very hard.
I also like art, you make wonderful cards.
In spelling, you copy down unusual words
And in your maths you count in your thirds.
Maybe our teacher will let us have a party
And maybe a new boy will come to school called Marti.

Will D'Costa (8)
St Christopher's RC Primary School, Codsall

Celebration

All friends gather round
Mums and dads too
Dad has got his drink
Mum has got hers
Here we go, 5, 4, 3, 2, 1.

Wow, a new millennium!
What will it bring?
New inventions?
Millennium Dome?

Happy millennium!

Liam Kilbane (8)
St Christopher's RC Primary School, Codsall

THE NEW MILLENNIUM

Well what do you know it's a new millennium tomorrow
Will we do old things a different way?
What things will be new?
What things should we remember?
Will we have parties in the streets?

What new things will be done?
Lot of new things to be won.
Will our parents get drunk at parties?
Or will they act like real smarties?
Now these are good questions to ask.

What new inventions will be made?
Will there be a millennium parade?
But will they remember what
Happened about 2000 years ago? I think not.

I know people will try to get into the Millennium Dome
I won't though.
But how much will it cost?
I don't have to worry, because I am not going.
I would rather go to parties.

I wonder if these questions will be answered
We will just have to wait and see.
So many questions to be answered
It's not that long to wait now,
Not long at all.

Edward Rogers (9)
St Christopher's RC Primary School, Codsall

MILLENNIUM

The Millennium. What does it mean to me?
Party, party, party,
That's how it will start for me.
Celebration with food, drink and music,
And my family with me.
We will sing, shout and dance about
From early evening on 31st December,
Until late in the day on the 1st January 2000.

How will we live in the Year 2000?
What will it be like?
Robots to work,
Humans to rest,
Remotes in our hand.
Holiday to the moon or Mars,
Get there by spaceship,
Robots drive.
It would take two days
But worth the wait
In the new millennium.

James Davies (8)
St Christopher's RC Primary School, Codsall

MILLENNIUM

How about if aliens landed on earth
and started communicating with us.

What if people who have already died came
back to life for a few days.

Wouldn't it be funny if men have babies?

What if animals could talk to us.

What about if plants came to life and
started eating things.

I would love to travel and explore the
world in just a few days on Concorde.

Kaleigh Diver (11)
St Christopher's RC Primary School, Codsall

COUNTDOWN TO THE MILLENNIUM

10, 9, 8, 7 . . . The clock's ticking down
I'm nosily jumping up and down.
The adults start to mumble,
My nan starts to frown
My little cousin's asleep already
Hugging her furry teddy.
6, 5, 4 . . . I'm starting to bite my fingernails
I'm starting to bite my lip
My heart's beating faster, my mind starts to flip.
I sink sleepily into my nan's lap, then I start to cry
I've got quite attached to this century
Don't let it pass by.
3, 2 . . . Stop!
The gentle rain starts to drop
One . . .What's happening
It's here! It's here!
The new millennium, my millennium
A new century and a new year.

Lauren Kavanagh (9)
St Christopher's RC Primary School, Codsall

Millennium Ideas

The millennium is a celebration of 1000 years,
A time full of joy and fun,
It's a great time for everyone.
With a fun new year about to begin
And a great party atmosphere in the air.

New ideas can be thought of,
Such as *super robots* to clean the house
Or even great shampoos to get rid of your lice!
Fascinating toys for all ages
I bet the inventors will get paid massive wages!

Wacky and weird inventions for all to use,
Like the *electronic flyer*
(but watch you don't blow the fuse).
Why not try the *super jet pack*
Be careful though, you may never come back!

These inventions are really cool,
They really are a major tool!
If you don't use them properly,
They will explode,
And will probably leave you with no home!

Matthew Acton (8)
St Christopher's RC Primary School, Codsall

How Will I Celebrate The Year 2000

I'm going to party till after midnight.
Let the millennium come in with a bang.
Let 1999 out with a cheer!
It's going to be really cool!

I'm going to eat lots of party food,
Like sausages, sandwiches, chicken and cake,
And lots of other goodies.

I want to visit the new Millennium Dome,
With my mum and dad and my older sister
Laura.

All the museums to visit the palace to see,
The inventions and new technology
Things in the present and things from the past
Will all make the millennium a thing of the past.

Hannah O'Shea (8)
St Christopher's RC Primary School, Codsall

Celebration Of Millennium

Oh I'm so happy, yes, yes, yes,
About a celebration quite near now.
Why it is the new millennium.
People so busy, just like buzzy little bees.
The streets are crowded with people shopping for the party.
Oh! The celebration's getting nearer and nearer.
There goes Easter, there goes Hallowe'en, now there goes Christmas!
3, 2, 1
Let's party!

Rose Lister (8)
St Christopher's RC Primary School, Codsall

MILLENNIUM

What could be invented in the millennium?
It could be a remote-control pencil!
Or maybe a talking window washer?
It could be absolutely anything!

Even though you can't tell the future,
You can just carry on guessing!
A new variety of car?
Whoosh! Rockets that travel really far!

Try inventing something yourself!
You'll need screws and cogs,
And definitely some wires
And, of course, a very clever brain!

Iain Olliver (9)
St Christopher's RC Primary School, Codsall

THINGS TO DO

There are lots of things to remember when we celebrate the year 2000.
Going to new places.
Seeing new faces.
Seeing new inventions.
People getting their pensions.
People getting drunk on a ship that sunk.
New rides coming out,
With people that shout.
People with fat cats
I can tell you the facts.
That is what the year 2000 is to remember.

Thomas Beavon (9)
St Christopher's RC Primary School, Codsall

MILLENNIUM

I'm so excited for the millennium is here,
There should not be any tears.
Lots of new things to do and see,
Oh how exciting it will be.

New toys, new games to play
And new food and drink.
Oh how much there will be to do and see.
I just can't wait for the millennium to come.

The millennium is finally here.
All the parties are very near.
But will the millennium really come?
Or is it just a joke to overcome?

Sarah Stowe (9)
St Christopher's RC Primary School, Codsall

WHAT WILL HAPPEN IN THE YEAR 2000?

What will happen in the year 2000?

What will happen in the year 2000?
There might be a new invention like beds at school
There might be a new invention that makes you feel cool in the summer
What will happen in the year 2000?
There might be people visiting mars
There might be bikes that go really fast
What will happen in the year 2000?
Just what will happen in the year 2000?
2000, 2000, 2000, 2000.

Emma Dunn (9)
St Christopher's RC Primary School, Codsall

THE YEAR 2000!

Everyone is very excited,
Because the millennium is nearly here.

So let's celebrate with family and friends
Food, drink, dance and sing.

The room is very colourful,
And the food it just tastes wonderful!

Let's have some fun
With all the people around us.

Soon the gate of the Dome will open
People will crowd around I bet.

I wonder what the Dome will be like,
What's the colour, what's the decoration?

Will it sparkle, will it be covered in colourful jewels.
I don't know. Do you?

Anyway just remember,
That it's Jesus who's giving us this year!

Victoria Hargrove (9)
St Christopher's RC Primary School, Codsall

THE MILLENNIUM

Who knows what the future holds.
Maybe people won't have colds.
Unsolved mysteries could be solved.
Most of the ice-caps could have dissolved.
And maybe people could live on the moon.
And robots could rule over us soon.
Aliens could invade the world.

People will be gasping for words
Computers could be at your desk.
Waiting to ask you what you want next.
Who knows what the future toys are.
Maybe we won't have fuming cars.
Who knows what the future will be.
I suppose we'll have to wait and see!

Matthew Kulyna (11)
St Christopher's RC Primary School, Codsall

MILLENNIUM

In the millennium everyone will be happy,
They'll say 'Order some food and make it snappy!'

In the millennium!

I think that my little home
might turn into a Millennium Dome!

In the millennium!

Could my mummy grow a beard
or something even more weird!

In the millennium!

Pets might find out they can talk,
and take their humans for a walk!

In the millennium!

Laura Peacock (9)
St Christopher's RC Primary School, Codsall

ALIENS V TONY BLAIR

Will the aliens invade Downing Street?
Will they defeat,
or will Tony Blair declare
honest to be fair.

Will the aliens think next year will be fine?
Or will they wait until their son is nine.
Will this year
be when Tony Blair will fear?

Will the aliens die?
Or will Tony Blair cry?
Could the aliens fly
Tony Blair would rather buy a pie.
Will this happen in the year 2000
or won't it?

Stephen Olliver (11)
St Christopher's RC Primary School, Codsall

THE YEAR 2000

It's the year 2000 today,
Hip, hip, hip, hooray!

Parties, cakes and so much more,
Games, toys, books and magic galore.

Laughter, fun and wonder in the air,
People cheering and singing without a care.
Once it's gone and the party's all done
All I have to do is wait until the year 2001!

Joseph Thompson (9)
St Christopher's RC Primary School, Codsall

THE NEW MILLENNIUM

Millennium Bug keep away,
As we party away the day.
Fireworks flying high,
Crackling and bursting in the sky.

What will happen during this year,
Could it be the year we all fear.
Will the Earth be a place where aliens roam.
While we all quake in our homes.

Will reproduction be reversed,
Or will everybody become cursed.
As we try to perfect the human race,
Many of us will be lost without grace.

Will racism become a thing of the past,
Will the remembrance of Stephen Lawrence last.
Colour, creed, does not matter,
We can all make racism shatter.

But as the millennium lurks ever nearer,
It will all become much clearer.
That there is lots of work to be done,
And when it comes, we can all have fun.

Laura Moss (10)
St Christopher's RC Primary School, Codsall

MILLENNIUM

Shall we know what is about in space.
Shall scientists ever inform us.
For all we know aliens could be plunging
towards us.

What will fashion become when the year
2000 approaches us?
Will we be wearing heels to the sky and
waving our fellow friends goodbye.
As we rise up high.

Will men have babies instead of women?
Or will it never change?
I don't think that men will do it,
so women are still top of the range.

Lyndsey Denning (10)
St Christopher's RC Primary School, Codsall

FLOWERS

My bear flowers
has many powers.
She walks through the air
styling her hair.
Her birthday will be on the 3rd May
it will be a lovely sunny day.
And this will be her poem:
Flowers the bear has many powers.
One of which is rare.
She can tie 100 knots
in her blonde coloured hair.

Emma Acton (11)
St Christopher's RC Primary School, Codsall

ALIENS

On the dark, dim, murky planet of *Sonner*.
There lives a *Fangtwisday*.
A big hairy, warty monster with lots of teeth.
He plans to take over the moon.
With a mighty mousetrap that will snap the globe in half.

On the muddy, watery, dark planet of *Zatar*.
There lives a *Dulartie* a thin, stiff, hard, round spotty creature.
That plans to take over the Earth.
To smash it with a big wooden hammer and haunt
everyone to death with its big ugly face.

On the bright, misty planet of *Raver*.
There lives a *Zoozlonger* a slimy gooey smelly
piece of jelly.
He plans to take over the sun.
To put out that fire once and for all
and get rid of that blazing ball of gas.
To eat it and crunch it and tear it to bits as its jelly
tum-tum would put out the flames.

So watch out in the year 2000.
We might be smashed by a big wooden hammer.
The moon could be snapped into two half pieces.
The sun could be eaten by the great fat blob.
Zoozlonger.
So beware, watch out when you're about and don't
get caught.
Beware! . . . Beware!

Katherine Aston (11)
St Christopher's RC Primary School, Codsall

A Normal Millennium
Day Gone Wrong

I wake up in the morning,
but before I start yawning,
I am catapulted out of bed,
into the dining room where I am fed,
By my robots who serve me,
From breakfast all the way to tea.

After breakfast I go out on the escalator path,
If you fall it's quite a laugh.
Then I get on the rocket bus,
Because it's solar powered, everyone makes a fuss.
The bus lifts off - here we go,
Now we're high no longer low.

The sun goes in and we're stuck in outer space,
What are we going to do?
Says the look on the bus driver's face.
Out of the bus window I stare,
To people who go out,
I shout 'Take care!'

It's a miracle, the sun came out,
Everyone's making a fuss and starting to shout.
Home now, we're on our way.
Three cheers for the sun, hooray, hooray, hooray.
Now we are going back,
I hope my robots got my sack.

I get to the bus stop and what do I see,
My robot with my sack for me.
I go along the escalator path to my house.
Out of my pocket jumps a pink alien mouse.
I go in my lift straight to bed,
'What a day you've had,' my robot said.

Emma Davies (10)
St Christopher's RC Primary School, Codsall

ROBOTS

Robots are fierce,
Robots like a fight.
Robots come out
In the middle of the night.

They gnash, they crash,
They whack, they smack.
They attack anything they see.

Their home is robot wars,
They have lots of fun.
Get to the exit door,
With a run, run, run.

If you don't
The punishment is death.
You won't have time.
To catch your breath.

So can you beat the robots,
That are designed to kill.
Or will you fall
To the pit of oblivion?

James Turner (10)
St Christopher's RC Primary School, Codsall

SHUTDOWN ZERO ZERO

Zero, zero reads the date
now it's too late!
They didn't believe it
not even a little bit!
I eat and destroy
suck up fun and joy.
When they turn on the machine
I get really mean!
'Oh no!' they say.
Because I will make them pay!
There's so much to be broken
I have spoken!
Do you know me yet?
You must've met
me - the biggest bad!
The scariest virus to make micro-men sad.
You should be hiding under a rug!
Who am I? The Millennium bug!

Vikki Brown (11)
St Christopher's RC Primary School, Codsall

HI-TECH

Faster, faster, cars are zooming
slower, slower the new year's looming.
More and more we're surfing the Net,
even at school - to my regret.
Where are the three Rs the whip and the cane
will these ever be around - again.

Our world is moving round so fast.
Oh my! The millennium is here at last.
Robots are doing all our work.
In cyber space travels Captain Kirk.
Where is all our old tradition.
Where we had to stop, look and listen!

Rachael Sharples (10)
St Christopher's RC Primary School, Codsall

ANIMALS IN THE YEAR 2000

Animals will talk
they will sit more than they walk.
The dog, cat, mouse, rat,
they will be the same.

They will sit on your lap
and pull off your cap.
What will happen then,
they will chew up my school pen.

I hope it is not true,
it could happen to me or you.
So watch the animals,
especially the ones that live in tunnels.

Victoria Marie Dunn (11)
St Christopher's RC Primary School, Codsall

TOYS

Will it be big?
Will it be small?
Will it be squashy?
It's a ball!

Will it be round?
Will it go low?
Will it be square?
It's a yo-yo!

Will it be stiff?
Will it be fed?
Will I find it in my bed?
It's ted!

Elizabeth Handley (11)
St Christopher's RC Primary School, Codsall

ONE DAY

One day I wished I would be writing.
If life stops getting in my way.
One day
At my desk
Pen in hand . . .
What should I write about?
I hear a tap at the door.
My mum shouts
'It's for you darling.'
That night, I hoped I'd be writing
One day
Some day
When life stops getting in my way.

Kyla Worrall (9)
St John's CE Primary School, Stafford

PLAYGROUND

Noisy, crowded
children everywhere.
Playing, walking,
children everywhere.
Running, screaming
children everywhere.
Shouting, arguing
children everywhere.
Skipping, kicking
children everywhere.
It suddenly goes quiet.
Where have they all gone?
They have gone away.
Silent and quiet
Shh, shh, shh!

Rhian Parry (11)
St John's CE Primary School, Stafford

MAD HOUSE

My house is mad
my brothers are bad.
My sister is cruel
I feel like a fool.
My mum is glad
but my dad is sad.
My grans are cool
my grandads drool.
My aunts are thick
and my uncles are strict.
It's just another mad house.

Vicky Ann Pickford (10)
St John's CE Primary School, Stafford

FRIENDS

Friends are all different
in all sorts of ways.
They bring out the good and bad in me
in just as many days.

There are secrets to tell
and games to be played.
Problems which are shared
leave me less afraid.

For friends are there to help
when you're feeling sad.
They bring smiles and laughter
which makes you feel good.

All my friends are important
they mean loads to me.
They're there to be shared
and lots of happiness to be.

Kiran Madzimbamuto-Ray (10)
St John's CE Primary School, Stafford

IMAGINE

Imagine a snail as tall as a nail,
Imagine a cat as flat as a mat,
Imagine a dolphin going golfing.
Imagine a fish making a wish,
Imagine a dog kissing a frog.
Imagine, imagine, imagine.

Hannah Crossett (9)
St John's CE Primary School, Stafford

THE ALIENS

The aliens came to Earth one day,
zooming from far away.
Coming from the spaceship high
came a blinding stream of light.
They sucked some trees up from there,
it blew really hard and rustled my hair.
But then I suddenly stopped,
I realised they had dropped.
I looked back out the window again,
they were in a box with a metal frame.
I suddenly felt a cold chill,
there were definitely aliens on that hill.
They climbed into their spaceship,
and then went back to planet Clip.

James Duckworth (9)
St John's CE Primary School, Stafford

TWINS

Twins are funny and silly
big eyes, small eyes.
Long hair, short hair.
Irritating, good
smart and dumb.
But are difficult to tell apart
when seen.
Look carefully.

Kerry Tutty (9)
St John's CE Primary School, Stafford

SPACE

I don't think much of space.
My friends don't agree;
They think it's ace.
If I was up there I would not see.

I wonder what there is in space.
Spaceships, aliens and rockets too.
Across the universe they race,
I think this is what they do.

They make their way to planet Mars
they clear everything in sight.
They speed across the sweeping stars
I think they give most things a fright.

Scott Weetch (11)
St John's CE Primary School, Stafford

CURLY WURLY

Little Curly Wurly was a talker.
Mercy me.
He chattered after breakfast and
he chattered after tea.
He chattered in the morning
he chattered in the night.
He chattered in the school, and
he chattered in a fight.
He chattered till his family was
almost driven wild!
Oh, little Curly Wurly was a
very tiresome child!

Emma Ludlow (11)
St John's CE Primary School, Stafford

DOUGHNUTS

Doughnuts, doughnuts
you just can't beat 'em.
Chocolate or custard
you've just got to eat 'em.
Sticky with sugar, tasty with toffee
a great little cake to have with your coffee.

Apple or raspberry
or jelly and blueberry.
Whenever you eat them
your belly feels merry.
Some have a hole some are just round
the sugar leaves a smile like a clown.

Bakeries and cafes
supermarkets and shops.
Lots of different flavours
with all coloured tops.
Doughnuts, doughnuts you know how to find them.
Walk past a shop and you can just smell 'em.

Alex Sandford (11)
St John's CE Primary School, Stafford

BROTHER

He can be a pain when
he makes stupid noises with
his aeroplane.
He asks me stupid questions
so I give him stupid suggestions.
However he is my brother.

Vanessa Youlden (10)
St John's CE Primary School, Stafford

MY PETS

My puppy is white
she is not very bright.
She doesn't know the difference
between left and right.

My guinea pig squeaks
she's not strong but weak.
She only comes out to nose and peek.

My bird is yellow
he doesn't sound like a violin or cello
nor does he shout and bellow.

My rabbit is white with spots of black.
Which run in a line down her back
but she doesn't run round a racing track.

My fish are dumb
they aren't much fun
but they're my dog's best chum.

Natalie Harrop (11)
St John's CE Primary School, Stafford

TWO DANCING DINOSAURS

Two dancing Dinosaurs rocking round the sun
one collapsed from sunstroke, then there was one.
One dancing Dinosaur hijacked a plane
flew to Alaska and was never seen again.

Daniel Boulten (10)
St John's CE Primary School, Stafford

MONSTER BROTHER

Brother monster, monster brother.
Screaming crying to his mother.
He, she or an it,
I need a baby-handling kit.
He killed my rabbit,
it's such a bad habit.
He shoved a pen right up its nose
then tried to cut off my dad's toes.
Sister, brother - what a pain.
Please let them go out
don't let it rain.
Brother monster, monster brother,
screaming crying to his mother.

William Riley-Gibson (10)
St John's CE Primary School, Stafford

THE MAN WHO WENT TO SEA

There was a man who went to sea.
Who's never even seen a tree.
He saw a flea
and dropped his key
which fell on his knee
and dropped in the sea.
And that's the man who went to sea.
Who saw a flea
and dropped his key
which fell on his knee
and dropped in the sea.

Jamie Tindall (10)
St John's CE Primary School, Stafford

FLOBBY BLOBBY

My name is Mr Blobby
and I can fit my legs around a trolley.
I sit at home, watching the telly.
while the house is smelly,
and I've got a big belly
which comes down to my welly.
And my belly is almost as fat as my 28 inch telly.
I must be the fittest in my street called Flobby.
And in my lobby
I have got another hidden tummy.
Which is also yummy
and it is my dummy.
That's why my friends call me Mr Blobby.

Idean Farshbaf (11)
St John's CE Primary School, Stafford

DELPHINE

Delphine had always been sinking
but then she got hit by lightning.
For all that gained
she had to be reigned
then she never came back again.

Anita was quite arresting
but then she was found resting
for all that she reigned
she did not gain
and then she went back to her grave.

Jemma Finlay (10)
St John's CE Primary School, Stafford

THE WITCH WHO FELL IN A DITCH

The witch who fell in a ditch
was very keen to itch.
The witch who fell in a ditch
decided to go to the doctors to get it fixed.
The doctor said 'I'm sorry old witch, I cannot get the itch fixed.'
So with that the witch had a fit and turned the poor old doctor
into a light switch.
So all the doctor does now is click, click and click.
On the way home the witch started to itch again.
So when she was itching she walked into a football pitch
and with that she fell into a muddy ditch.
Never to be seen again!

Emily Clapham (8)
St John's CE Primary School, Stafford

A NICE CUP OF TEA

The kettle's boiled nice and hot
then you put it in the pot.
Get the cups, mind the pups
fetch the milk, don't spill the milk.
Get the biscuits and some guests.
Let the guests have a rest
and let them say
that's a nice cup of tea!

Leona Jones-Keating (11)
St John's CE Primary School, Stafford

AT THE MATCH

At the
match the team
score and the other
team swore. In the crowd
there was a fat chap who
started a scrap which ended with him
black and blue. There was another goal as
the team roared while the other team snored.
After the match there was a loud hooray followed
by a buffet. At the bar there was a car
that went through the bar. The
guy was quite shy but
in jail he had
lots of mail.
That was what happened at the match.

James Hodson (9)
St John's CE Primary School, Stafford

TEACHERS

Teachers, teachers are not fair.
Teachers, teachers do not care.
We have to go out and play
but they can always stay.
We have to run, run, run
but where is the sun, sun, sun?
When it's time to go in
they say 'Line up by the bin.'
So teachers, teachers are not fair
and teachers, teachers do not care.

Sahar Shahid Nadeem (11)
St John's CE Primary School, Stafford

BOOK FAIRS

I like book fairs.
You are allowed to go in pairs.
If you don't like books you should go in
If you dare.
And you can't have books to share.

It starts at half-past two.
If you bought a book, don't throw a shoe.
Or try to say 'Shoo!'

It finishes at a quarter-past four.
If you don't buy a book, you'll bang into a door.
Or into a wall.

It is at school for five days long.
If you don't go, you'd better write a song.
I don't care if you do a pong!

Helen Dean (10)
St John's CE Primary School, Stafford

FISHES

Fishes in the sea
fishes in the sea
what can you see?

Fishes in the sea
fishes in the sea
are swimming with me.

Fishes in the sea
fishes in the sea
are having tea!

Danielle Bridgland (9)
St John's CE Primary School, Stafford

FOSTER THE GIANT

I knew a giant called Foster.
He lived in the city of Gloucester.
He was stumping around one day
eating everything in his way.
First the trees
then the bees.
He swam in rivers
and the cold ones gave him shivers.
Even though he was big
he loved playing tig.
And then he stamped on the vicar's wig.
Foster ran and ran
and met his friend Dan.
Dan was very sporty,
his lucky number was forty.
One day he came round my house,
and saw my pet mouse,
and he ran out of the house!
Foster loved playing with his cat,
and sometimes hid it in his hat.
The cat catches the rats,
and scares away the bats.
Finally at the end of the day,
Foster lies down in the hay,
to wake up the next day
to have more fun and play.
Giant Foster is very tall
but never bangs into the wall.
So that's about giants and all!

Sarah Rizeq (8)
St John's CE Primary School, Stafford

THE FAST PENGUIN

Go, go penguin, running fast,
jumps over a lump of grass.
Go, go penguin running fast,
skids past a football mast.

Go, go penguin, running fast
tries to tell the weather forecast.
Go, go penguin, running fast
jogging on a wooden plank.

Go, go penguin running fast
dives on a blast of the England mast.
Go, go penguin running fast,
races round Chelsea's ground.

Come on penguin, it's time to go
you must be worn out after
that go go going.

Andrew Gallear (9)
St John's CE Primary School, Stafford

THE SEA

I've seen the sea so far away, roaring and
soaring, splashing and crashing.
Night to day, day to night.
Never going to stop, never going to go away.
Never going to cease to rain.
Oh why oh why, on my holiday,
will it never stop or go away?

Kyle James Smith (11)
St John's CE Primary School, Stafford

SEASONS

In the summer
it is funnier.
Because there is hardly a storm
and there are lots of fields with corn.
I can go to the beach
and there is a juicy apple,
I cannot reach.

In autumn
I get very bored.
Leaves fall on the ground
and make a funny sound.
It is quite cold
so flowers can die and fold.

In winter
I get an ice-splinter.
Then I build a snowman
then it melts as if it's been in a hot pan.
I wear warm clothes
and I get dead toes.

In spring
I go and ping.
All the leaves and buds have grown
and seeds are sown.
The sky is clear
and the moon is seen as a sphere.

Megan Preece (10)
St John's CE Primary School, Stafford

FOOTBALL

Football is fun
even in summer
especially in goal
where you don't run around.

I love to dive
and run and jump.
The feeling of the ball in my arms
is so amazing I don't mind the pain.

I love to score
but not to end up on the floor.
To tackle and run
scoring is fun.

Damon Morbey (9)
St John's CE Primary School, Stafford

RED

Thank you dragons,
thank you, thank you dragons.
For the heat and meat, thank you.
Thank you, thank you for your intelligent feet.
Dragons, dragons on the rooftops.
Dragons, dragons in the cave.
There's a dragon in my bedroom.
So thank you, thank you God
for the dragon in the fog. Dragons
Dragons give us a fight but then they
frighten you and make your hair
stick up.

Joshua Baker (8)
St John's CE Primary School, Stafford

IF YOU SEE ME

If you see me walking down the street.
Please don't look at my feet
because they're so big you know.
And I'm not saying anything about
my big toe.

If you see me walking down town
please don't look at my gown.
Because it's not so pretty
which is a pity.

If you see me in the city
please make sure I don't trip over
my kitty.
Because if I do
I'll blame it all on you.

Emma Jane Siggery (11)
St John's CE Primary School, Stafford

EGYPTIAN NIGHTS

The light
of the moon, lights
up the silvery skies of
Egypt on those cold and chilly nights.
People sleep on the top of building rooftops and
Pharaoh's dine in style with food and drink from miles
around. Best of all the Gods are watching over Egypt.

Jack Davis (9)
St John's CE Primary School, Stafford

MY MEMORIES

My memories can be said,
My memories can be happy,
My memories can be whatever I want them to be,
My memories can be long,
My memories can be short,
My memories can be strong,
My memories can be weak,
My memories, my memories.

Christopher Fox (10)
St John's CE Primary School, Stafford

A SPRING POEM

As I walked down to school one day.
I met a bird on his way.
He sang a song so nice and sweet
because the sun shone on his beak.
The song echoed around the playground wall
and followed us into the school hall.

Samantha Butt (8)
St John's CE Primary School, Stafford

UNDER THE SEA

Dolphins are jumping out of the sea.
Fish is what they like for tea.
Whales echo as loud as they can.
Of course they don't use a frying pan.
Crabs crawl sideways, they pinch your nose
and they pinch your toes.

Louise Brandrick (8)
St John's CE Primary School, Stafford

THE FLOWER LADY

Flowers from the flower lady
like daffodils and tulips
of every smell and colour.
Well any flower you adore
everyone hung on her front door.
Reading about every flower
in your special book.

Lace tied round the bridal tree
and everyday snap-dragons around.
Did you guess who it is?
Yes! It's the flower lady.

Deven Morton (8)
St John's CE Primary School, Stafford

TOFFEE CRISP

You open the packet you can smell the sweetness
as you put your sharp teeth into it.
It's munchy and you can hear it munching
in your mouth.
You can taste the lovely flavour of sweet chocolate,
you spread it on your tongue.
Toffee Crisp. Toffee Crisp
when you see Toffee Crisp
it makes your mouth water.
Toffee Crisp. Toffee Crisp.

Ben Fleming (9)
St John's CE Primary School, Stafford

THE LAND OF EGYPT

In the land of Egypt it's hot and dry.
Long hard days working under the golden sun.
Golden sun. Golden sun.
Slaves slaving for the Pharaohs
building pyramids and fetching rocks
while the Pharaoh dines in style.
Golden sun. Golden sun.
Farmers plough their fields
waiting for the Nile to flood.
Golden sun. Golden sun.
Cattle take people to market
to sell their crops.
Golden sun. Golden sun.

Joe Murray (9)
St John's CE Primary School, Stafford

IN THE SEA

In the sea you can see
fish and fins and dolphins.
Diving high, diving low.
Dolphins, dolphins, please don't go.
In the sea you can see
shells and seahorses.
On the top of the sand surface.
In the sea, you can see
the water still for evermore.

Liz Howard (8)
St John's CE Primary School, Stafford

GOLDEN SEAGULLS

Golden seagulls, golden seagulls,
flying over the golden sea.
In the winter they fly south.
In the summer they fly west.
Golden seagulls, golden seagulls,
flying over the golden sea.
You can see them on the beach
sometimes standing on a rock.
Golden seagulls, golden seagulls
flying over the golden sea.
Sometimes walking.
Sometimes flying.
Upon the cliff and the sea.

David Bufton (9)
St John's CE Primary School, Stafford

MY MUM IS THE BEST

My mum is the best.
she has a cosy house like a nest.
My mum is the best
she never has a rest.
My mum is the best
she gives me a spelling test.
My mum is the best
she never makes me wear a vest.

Kathryn Brophy (9)
St John's CE Primary School, Stafford

IF YOU SMELL

If you smell my flower
you will get awesome power.
And then you can fly up in the sky
like a dragonfly.

If you smell my socks
you will get the chicken pox.
Then you'll go insane,
and be in great pain.

If you smell my dog
you'll turn into a frog.
My dog's name is Smelly
and he has a big belly.

Rachel Cawley (10)
St John's CE Primary School, Stafford

DOLPHINS

Dolphins, dolphins
swim through the sea.
See their long fin
splash at me.
Dolphins, dolphins
swim through the long blue sea.
Watch them as they
swim with me.
Dolphins, dolphins
gaze at the sun.

Victoria Philp (8)
St John's CE Primary School, Stafford

THE FAMILY JEWELLERY

The family jewellery has been passed down to me.
It has been through all my family tree.
When I'm old I will pass it down.
So that with beauty my children I'll crown.

The jewellery is so beautiful, it is gold, silver
and brown and all the different colours are
as amazing as my crown.
I have got earrings, rings and all different things.
I have got a necklace, a bracelet and anklet too.
But I never wear them when I'm going to my aunts
because she always takes them away, I glance.

Sarah Woodward (10)
St John's CE Primary School, Stafford

WHEN MY FACE WAS RED

One Monday morning I couldn't get out of bed.
My face had gone red. Yes red!
I had a wash then put make-up on
but the redness still hadn't gone!
My mum said that I couldn't go to school.
Or for my daily swim at the swimming pool.
The next morning I got out of bed
and my face was no longer red!
So quickly I got ready for school
after that I went to the swimming pool.

Lindsey Walkeden (11)
St John's CE Primary School, Stafford

THE CATERPILLAR

I know a caterpillar
and his name is Fred.
He's been around for twenty years
and will not go to bed.

This little caterpillar
who will not go to bed.
Once built himself a cocoon
but then out popped his head.

I thought he had changed
into a butterfly.
But then he said 'What's the point?
I'm soon going to die.'

Hannah Clark (11)
St John's CE Primary School, Stafford

IN THE MIDDLE OF THE END

In the middle of the end
a man went straight round the bend.
A horse flew over the moon,
and a boy floated on a balloon.
Then a knight in shining armour
rode a board around the harbour.
Then a couple walking to town,
stepped on King Henry's crown!

Richard Cropper (11)
St John's CE Primary School, Stafford

ASSASSINS

They're always in the dark
lighting a spark
that you and me can't see.
Height you must like
you have to bike
and keep going no matter what.
You have to cope with danger
and with weapons you're no stranger.
You must not just fade
or blend in with the shade.
You must kill
and stay so still.
And be able to creep
and never sleep.
For the world that you overcome.

Andy Pringle (10)
St John's CE Primary School, Stafford

PETER SCHMEICHEL

Peter Schmeichel fell on the floor
and let the other team Stoke City score
then he lost his job and he was poor.
And then he went to the ref and swore
and then he broke the football laws.
Stoke City tackled the ball
and then it was a handball.
Peter asked for his job back
'Only if you don't fall on the floor.'

James Ludlow (8)
St John's CE Primary School, Stafford

AT THE MATCH

At the match they scored a goal.
At the match they went yippee.
In the stadium they all cheered
while the other team sneered.
In the crowd there was a fat chap
who started a fight and ended up
crying all the way home.
There was a referee who looked very nice
but he started a fight and broke the law
and got thrown out of the stadium with him
very embarrassed.
At the end they went to the pub to celebrate.
With them all drunk it looks
like they might have a fight.

Andrew Oldham (9)
St John's CE Primary School, Stafford

TIME

Time in many ways is like water
coming and going in deepest wonder.
And in the darkness of the night
the tide on the sand is so tight.

Time in many ways causes strife
day in day out throughout our life.
From when we are born, to the day that we die
time will go with us into the sky.

Holly Buckless (11)
St John's CE Primary School, Stafford

THE RAT IN MY HAT

There's a rat, in my hat
what shall I do?
I'll get a cat.
I went to my neighbour
to ask for a favour.
I said I need a cat
for the rat in my hat.
My neighbour said scat for
I haven't got a cat
for the rat in your hat.
But you could phone Matt
because he's got a cat
that could eat a whole rat.
At last Matt was here
or else he was near.
He was outside the door
standing like a bore
with a cat in his hand.
I let him in, giving his cat a ride
the cat pounced out looking for its
pride. I showed it the hat
so he pounced in the hat
licking its lips it gobbled up the rat.
It was gone forever
never seen again.
I could wear my hat
without that stupid rat.

Scott Haley (9)
St John's CE Primary School, Stafford

THE DRAGON

The dragon was green with lumpy spots,
It had big feet with dark brown claws,
It headed towards the Townsville park,
And squashed the swings and the slide.
Then it headed towards my house,
And startled my mum, who cried,
And I just said *'My gum!'*

Kim Rushworth (10)
St John's CE Primary School, Stafford

IMAGINE

Imagine if I was a butterfly, I would fly high in the sky.
Imagine if I was a duck, I would love to play in the muck.
Imagine if I was a clock, I would go tick-tock, tick-tock.
Imagine if I was the sun I would have fun, fun, fun.

Donna Owen (11)
St John's CE Primary School, Stafford

TREES

Trees, trees are everywhere,
Leaves, leaves blowing here and there,
Breeze blows the branches around,
The birds build their nests,
The pink blossom flowering.

Peter Whyman (9)
St John's CE Primary School, Stafford

No Longer

'What?'
Tears fill my eyes.
I can't believe the person I knew so well
and loved,
Is no longer here.
And now, no longer any hugs or kisses
or even conversation.
The phone in the house no longer rings,
there is no one to answer it.
The bed lies empty,
there is no one to fill it.
The food is uneaten,
there is no one to eat it.
The picture hangs on the wall,
but there is no one to see it.
The old lady is dead.

Dead.

Matthew Tyzack (11)
St John's CE Primary School, Stafford

My Zit

I have a planet on my face.
I think it's come from outer space.
Mirror, mirror on the wall - should I call the doc at all?

It could be infected
or it could be inspected.
Or there could be no life at all.

Gurdev Gill (10)
St John's CE Primary School, Stafford

THE FAMILY TEENAGER!

In my family there are four people.
Two are adults and one a child.
The fourth is a teenager who can go wild
Who likes to drink her tea all mild.

We have a cat and a bird
she tries to teach the bird a word.
The cat just sits around all day
Unless the girl decides to play.

She gets the string and starts to throw.
The cat gets annoyed with her so.
She decides to get off the back of the chair
and attacks the girl's legs when she's unaware.

Philippa Wimpory (11)
St John's CE Primary School, Stafford

BOB'S LIFE

There was a man called Bob,
Who didn't really like his job.
He watched the TV every night,
After that, he had a fight,
His wife didn't put up with this,
She ran away without a kiss.
Then poor Bob, he too ran away,
And was never seen until today.
He was found by the police,
Sadly, he wasn't in one piece.
His wife came back not knowing his fate,
She became mental. Boy, was it too late.

Michael Jones (11)
St John's CE Primary School, Stafford

THE CAT'S EYES

The cat sits on the wall at night,
Eyes awonder, shining bright,
Staring up into the starry sky,
Watching as the time goes by.

The cat still sitting on the wall,
Each eye like a crystal ball,
Deep and magical through and through,
Glistening, glinting, good as new.

Without a sound the cat falls asleep,
Goodbye to the eyes, so dark, so deep,
The morning comes, the eyes shut tight,
Waiting for the next dark night.

Sally Ecclestone (11)
St John's CE Primary School, Stafford

FRED THE FISH

Poor little Fred, the fish,
All he did was sit in his favourite dish,
Until one day a net came and he didn't know what to do,
He sat in his dish and started to cry,
He wept and he wept 'I'm going to die, I'm going to die.'
Too late he got caught in the net and pulled out of the water,
All he could see was boys.
Boy, fish all I can say is hate!
Huh! It's little enough to use as bait,
Come on, let's go and find something *bigger.*

Emily Swales (11)
St John's CE Primary School, Stafford

160

MY MUM

Now I'm young again, I feel,
I know ghosts are not real,
My mum disagrees with me,
I got sent to my room, you see.

When I came out,
My mum said she was sorry,
And agreed to go out for a back-to-back curry,
Now we're friends again.

My mum is the best you know,
My brother loves her too,
So that means that she is the best
Person I ever knew.

Robert Fowler (10)
St John's CE Primary School, Stafford

MY PET PANDA

I had a pet panda, I called it Miranda,
I tried to teach it how to jump, but it wouldn't move,
The big, fat lump.

I tried to teach it how to ride a bike,
But it just lay there,
Like a pike.

But then one day there came a knock,
It was a man selling a clock,
He saw Miranda, my panda, and took her away,
I've never seen her since that day.

Rebecca Revell (11)
St John's CE Primary School, Stafford

IMAGINE

Imagine a cat as small as a rat,
Imagine a snake tall, round and fat,
Imagine a giraffe with a very short neck,
Imagine a woodpecker unable to peck.

Imagine at night it looked so bright,
Imagine that day had become night,
Imagine a second as long as a day,
Imagine what everybody would say.

Imagine your mum was your dad,
Imagine, would it be that bad,
Imagine the summer without no sun,
Imagine that it would be no fun.

Imagine, imagine, imagine.

Holly Dunkley (10)
St John's CE Primary School, Stafford

DREAM MAKERS

I would like to meet the dream makers,
The people who make our dreams.
They make us laugh and sometimes scream,
We can do anything in our sweet dreams,
We can fly like birds in the sky,
We can run mile after mile,
In some people's dreams knights battle knights,
In some people's dreams it's fight after fight,
And when I wake up from another dream,
I thank my imagination for creating the scene.

Darryll Johns (10)
St John's CE Primary School, Stafford

LITTLE AND LARGE

Just imagine if a snail was the size of a whale,
I think it would look funny and go pale.
Just imagine if an elephant was the size of worm,
It would have big, fat feet and it would not squirm.
And if a human turned into an ant,
We would never run fast and never, ever pant.

Matthew Gollins (10)
St John's CE Primary School, Stafford

RONALDO

Ronaldo is the best player in the world,
He plays for Inter Milan and he plays
For an international side called Brazil.
The teams he plays for are all sponsored by Nike,
Nike pays him to wear his football boots.

Scott Roebuck (10)
St John's CE Primary School, Stafford

BOOKS

Books are the best,
Better than all the rest,
I read every day,
It's better than TV,
Not as good as tea,
But books are great.

Nicholas Sandiford (9)
St John's CE Primary School, Stafford

MICE

I think mice
Are rather nice,
They have long tails,
They have faces that are small,
Mice have not got any,
Chins at all.
Their ears are pink,
Their teeth are white,
They run about,
The strangest house at night,
They nibble things that,
They should not touch,
And no one seems,
To like them much,
But did you know,
I think that mice,
Are very nice.

Rachel Lawson (9)
St John's CE Primary School, Stafford

ONCE A LITTLE BABY

There was once a lady,
Who had a baby,
She called it Rose,
Who always had a runny nose,
She took her to see the doctor,
Who said 'You need to rock her,'
She went to the nurse,
Then suddenly she went with a burst.

Sarah Healy (10)
St John's CE Primary School, Stafford

FRIENDS

I have lots of friends, big and thin,
But I have never thrown one in the bin,
I tried, I tried to put one down the loo,
But she popped back up and said *'Boo!'*

One day after school I was raving mad,
I took one to market and sold her to a lad,
That day I went home, I jumped on my throne,
And said thank goodness she's gone,
That very second there was a tap at the door
He said 'I don't want her anymore.'
'I'm back' she shouted with a bang, with lots more,
After all, what are friends for.

Jodie Warner (10)
St John's CE Primary School, Stafford

IN SPACE

Five, four, three, two, one *blast-off.*
Off we go into space,
At a really fast, tremendous pace,
As we go past the planets,
We see little aliens having a race.
When we went to Pluto,
It was far too cold, and my captain said
'How many times have you been told!'
When we went past the sun,
Me and my crew burnt like a bun.
So we went back to Earth,
And landed on soft, bouncy turf.

Robert Reading (10)
St John's CE Primary School, Stafford

MY DAD PAUL

My dad Paul is five feet tall,
And he's round like a beach ball.
My dad Paul is not very tall,
And he hates playing football.
I love my dad,
But sometimes he gets mad,
And he makes me very sad.

Scott Randles (10)
St John's CE Primary School, Stafford

DOLPHINS

Dolphins are dolphins, cute as can be,
They swim about all day in the sea,
Dolphins are restless, they eat fish from your hand,
They glide above water as well as the sand,
Dolphins can swim, over ten feet,
They will see each other and then they will meet.

Peter Jones (8)
St John's CE Primary School, Stafford

FISHES

I am a fish and perhaps rather small,
But not like a shrimp or a tiddler,
And more, I live in a beautiful lake,
Each day growing bigger.
Down in the depth of the blue, grey and green.

Laura Teitge (9)
St John's CE Primary School, Stafford

FINGERS AND DOORS DON'T GO TOGETHER

Fingers and doors don't
Go together
Because
When you trap
Your finger
In a door
The usual
Thing to
Do
Is jump up and
Down
But
Don't swear
If you swear
It hurts
Much more
So what do
You do when you
Trap your
Finger in the door
Jump up and
Down
And say
Dash

Kate Bufton (9)
St John's CE Primary School, Stafford

THE SNAIL

This very large but brown snail,
Is as tall as a nail,
And hates rain and hail,
He hates people who wail,
And hates the person who delivers the mail,
He hates the wind and gales,
And hates hay bales,
He likes to bake,
Yummy jam cake,
He likes to swim in the lake,
And his best friend is called Jake,
Sometimes he likes to go to sleep,
Sometimes he likes to stay awake,
He has a 4x4 Jeep,
And at the age of ninety-four,
He sadly dropped dead to the floor,
Because of old age.

Luke Mudford (10)
St John's CE Primary School, Stafford

FRED AND HIS BED!

I've got a friend and his name is Fred,
He absolutely loves his bed,
One day he brought it into school,
Everyone laughed and called him a fool.
One day when Fred was getting old,
His bed was taken to a shop and sold,
Fred cried and cried all day,
And then said 'It's only a bed anyway!'

Robert Senior (10)
St John's CE Primary School, Stafford

THE BIN MONSTER

I go to put something
In the bin,
I know what's going
To happen.

You open the bin,
And there inside, (he will give you a surprise),
Is the big,
Hairy, ugly,
Bin monster.

I am creeping closer now,
And closer and I am,
Just about to open the bin.
And it's gone. Oh no.

Lorna Perry (10)
St John's CE Primary School, Stafford

THE FOOTBALL MATCH

When we lose in the freezing cold frost,
I always go home and sulk for half an hour,
And of course my dad says 'You've just got to
Face it, either win or lose.'
Sometimes, you've got to lose but,
Why have I got to lose,
Why can't I win?
Then it was my day,
I scored my first hat-trick,
And my friend did too,
Then I said to myself,
It doesn't matter if I win or lose.

Matthew Suffolk (9)
St John's CE Primary School, Stafford

MY DOG

My dog, he acts like a big, gigantic hog,
He's not like any other kind of dog.
He looks really, really weird,
He looks like he's got a beard.

He always takes all of my bed,
But then I say I'll have your head.
My dog is really dumb,
but he won't have any fun.

He's always in a big mood,
But he's not when he eats food.
He's really my best friend,
But I don't want this trouble to end.

Patrick Durie (9)
St John's CE Primary School, Stafford

DOLPHINS

Dolphins swim and play,
In the sunset is what I say,
Through the water they glide,
But sometimes they slide.

They play in the morning sun,
But sadly, they can't run,
They are grey,
But can't bray.

They elegantly jump,
And land with a thump,
They slowly sway,
Then swim away.

Seonaid Fleming (10)
St John's CE Primary School, Stafford

THE SUN

The sun shines down on the earth
the nature glimmering in the sunlight.
The sun shines on the rainbow
feeling like never before.

Another day . . . another night.

The sun is set into darkness
the oceans start to shine.
The sun gets deeper and deeper
the forest gets darker and darker.

Another day . . . another night.

The sun is setting in the sky
the moon comes out.
There is still a light
it is the moon still showing the sun.

Another day . . . another night!

Darren Rogers (11)
St Joseph & St Theresa's RC Primary School, Burntwood

THE WEATHER

The shining sun shines its spectacular rays
through the frosty air, giving light to the world.
The darkness of the world is enlightened
by its staggering power.

The wind goes whizzing by
whooshing and pushing low and high.
Destroying and carrying objects in its path
nothing will survive - not one thing!

Dominic Parsons (11)
St Joseph & St Theresa's RC Primary School, Burntwood

LONELINESS

As I walk through the sandy plain
all I see are the waves splashing
against the silky shore.

I hear the echo of distant voices
blowing in the wind.
The sadness comes back to me
as I feel the loneliness inside of me.

I feel like my soul has left
then the dark shadows lurk upon me.
I know that the only friend to look
over me is God . . .
He is my Creator, who will
keep despair at bay.

Kyle Ball (11)
St Joseph & St Theresa's RC Primary School, Burntwood

SPRING

Spring is a time of new growth
the birds whistle and sing on the new buds.
The horns on the daffodils blow in the breeze
the days grow longer and the nights grow short.

The sky is painted at springtime
when the stars are scattered in the sky.
We think about our God who is watching -
looking after the people who have
gone before us . . .

Darren Hames (11)
St Joseph & St Theresa's RC Primary School, Burntwood

TO BE DEAF

The world encloses my being;
should you not appreciate
how fortunate you are?
Hark! Are you able to hear
other's conversing?
To be able to hear . . .
To be able to hear . . .

The world is muffled
in memory to me.
Lifeless to me . . .
All I can depend on
is my sight.
But to be deaf is anxiety
and terror forever.

I have often wondered
what it's like to hear.
But losing your hearing gradually
is worse, and I've often wondered
what it's like to hear . . . to hear . . .
to hear.

Rebecca Ward (10)
St Joseph & St Theresa's RC Primary School, Burntwood

THE SEA

The soft silky blue sea flushes
the hard grey pebbles away.

An instant breeze comes brushing past
the sun is shining before me.
I feel the Lord is here.

Andrea Jagielski (11)
St Joseph & St Theresa's RC Primary School, Burntwood

THE SUN IS SHINING

The sun is shining on the shimmering sea
the silver foam bouncing off the rocks.
The palm trees sway to the gentle breeze
on the sandy shore.

The ivory rocks stand proud and tall
as the waves dance around them.
The seagulls sing in the sky above
as they glide around.

The sun goes down
and the silence sets
as the shadows move in closer.
Another day ends - tomorrow a new beginning.

Kimberley Rogers (11)
St Joseph & St Theresa's RC Primary School, Burntwood

THE SUN

Looking at the radiant sunshine before me
it stands out with strength and stamina.
It reflects back to me like a moonlit mirror
The sun's like joy that goes throughout the land.

The nights come by and the sun dies down
the darkness overcomes the land.
all to guide me is the moonlit stars.
The stars are like joy that goes throughout the land.

Luke Service (11)
St Joseph & St Theresa's RC Primary School, Burntwood

THE GARDEN OF EDEN

I know that I am soon to go
but before I do I will live
in awe and wonder.

The blooming flowers of spring
are the colours of the rainbow.
The scents that stole my heart
are still remembered in my nose.

I am walking, walking towards the light
but I still have far to go (it's the pitch of night).

It's summer now - and the radiant and beaming sun
is shining its hardest.
Spring caterpillars are butterflies.
The leaves and life is back once more
in this is now a thriving place.

Aiden McNamara (10)
St Joseph & St Theresa's RC Primary School, Burntwood

THE WORLD BEYOND

A radiant day it was to thee
My joy burst out
To the world beyond.
An autumn day had just begun.
The radiant sun sparkled on the water's edge.
Adam and Eve reached forth
For the forbidden apple . . . !

Amy Wicks (10)
St Joseph & St Theresa's RC Primary School, Burntwood

THE WORLD

The world is round and wide
with fascinating and passionate colours.
The sky is a brilliant breathtaking blue
and the grass is a glamorous gangster green
with the sea that is any glittering shade
of green or shadowy blue.

The world has many things to show
the slimy and slithery snakes, or maybe
the big brown bears.
The fabulous flocks of flowers, or maybe
the tremendously tall trees.

Jason Upton (11)
St Joseph & St Theresa's RC Primary School, Burntwood

THE SEA

As I ramble over the sandy beach
the waves lap to and fro.
They come and saturate the sand
then drift back to sea.

I see people swimming
as I smell the salty water.
The sun shining down
as the water shines and gleams.

Kristine Chandler (10)
St Joseph & St Theresa's RC Primary School, Burntwood

AUTUMN AND WINTER

The glorious autumn morning
the air as fresh as milk.
The warm breeze hits my face as delicate as it can
as I walk across my garden. I crush the crisp golden leaves.
I carry on walking until I come to a windswept tree,
evacuated with leaves except for broken pieces of bark.

The cruel bleak weather
the wind as cold as snow.
I walk along the road
feeling like an ice cube.
There's no sight of leaves
the wind must have swept them away!

James Pearson (11)
St Joseph & St Theresa's RC Primary School, Burntwood

A MID-SUMMER'S DAY

As I was walking through the astounding forest
on a mid-summer's day.
I suddenly caught a glimpse of a beautiful tulip
glittering in the radiant sunlight.
I looked up at the crystal-blue sky.
There was not a cloud in sight.

Cascading through the sky were dark storm-clouds
about to burst open with rain.
I ran to take shelter under a rock
it was like a big hollow cavern.

Victoria Anne Smith (11)
St Joseph & St Theresa's RC Primary School, Burntwood

DEAFNESS

As I sit on a cold dense chair
I watch children playing
but I cannot hear them.
Every day of my life
spent watching
but not hearing.

When you're deaf
the loneliness prowls around.
But you know it's the way God made you.
He made each one of us differently,
no one is the same.

I will never be different - I will never hear!
But I know God loves me forever and ever.

Jennifer Ralphs (11)
St Joseph & St Theresa's RC Primary School, Burntwood

THE SEA

As I walked towards the blue flowing sea
the waves all around me.
As they cascade onto the sandy shore
the fascinating colours surround me.

The sea is all different shades of blue
the large waves fill the sandy shore.
No more glistening sand to be seen
my voice starts to fade.

Sofie Leroux (10)
St Joseph & St Theresa's RC Primary School, Burntwood

WOLF'S DINNER

Three little piglets went out to play
one made a house out of hay.
Another made a house out of sticks
but the cleverest built his of bricks.

The wolf went to the house out of hay
he knocked on the door and say 'You hey!'
Now that little piggy was rather shy
Wolf said 'Open up! Or you'll soon die!'

By that time the pig was getting jumpy
the wolf was ready for a pig that was big and lumpy.
At this time the pig gave up
the wolf came in and drank him as sup.

The wolf was still hungry, so he hunted for more.
He sniffed around and ended up at the other pig's door.
The wolf overheard the pig's plan
the pig was going to run to his Nan.

So the wolf knocked the door down and saw the pig stand.
He gobbled the pig up and said 'That wasn't very grand!'
The wolf was still hungry so he sniffed for some more
and came across an apple core.

He was just going off for his date,
but he spotted another pig that he hadn't yet ate.
The wolf had a really cunning plan
He would dress up as the little pig's Nan.

The wolf went over to that little pig,
and said 'Dear darling, do you like my new wig?'
The wolf ate the pig with a little bit of spice
but all it needed with it
was a little bit of rice!

Jordan Blake (9)
St Joseph & St Theresa's RC Primary School, Burntwood

ME AND DADDY

Up on daddy's shoulders
having so much fun.
Up on daddy's shoulders
eating a hot-cross bun.

In the water with daddy
pull me under the water.
In the water with daddy
my daddy said 'Caught her.'

Daddy said 'It's time to go.'
And wrapped a towel around me.
Daddy said 'It's time to go,'
and sneaked up behind me.

Caitlin Grainger (9)
St Margaret's CE Junior School, Newcastle-under-Lyme

SPORTS DAY

Children running
        Parent's clapping
                Sister's screaming
        Brother's howling
                Teacher's shouting
        Kid's jumping
Boy's skipping
        Girl's throwing
                Teacher's awarding

People going

Jessica Ann Crooks (9)
St Margaret's CE Junior School, Newcastle-under-Lyme

THE SEA IS LIKE . . . ?

The sea is like a big brown bear
roaring with all its might.
It lashes against the cliffs
all through the day and night.

The sea is like a cruel coyote
scratching against the sands.
It stands there howling day and night
attacking harbour hands.

The sea is like a wicked wolf
pulling boats underneath.
It pulls them down so far
they reach the coral reef.

The sea is like an angry eagle
sharp-eyed and witty.
It soars around the sandy cliffs
waiting for its tea.

Stephen Jackson (9)
St Margaret's CE Junior School, Newcastle-under-Lyme

THE SEA

The sea splashing on beaches.
Children splashing in the sea.
The waves moving everywhere.
The sea's everywhere.

Children swimming in the sea.
People surfboarding in the sea.
The sea so deep and blue.
The sea is fun.

Richard Simpson
St Margaret's CE Junior School, Newcastle-under-Lyme

THE SEA

The sea is very big
it surrounds us every day.

Ships sail on it
fish swim in it.

It comes upon the sandy shores
splashing on the sand.

Never getting bigger, never getting smaller.
The waves splashing seaweed right upon the shore.

Now it's getting dark
the tide is going further back.

Seaweed stays on the beach.
The fish go back as well.

Matthew Fernyhough (8)
St Margaret's CE Junior School, Newcastle-under-Lyme

IN THE SWIMMING POOL

Children jumping,
   Mum's watching,
     Friend's shouting,
       Lifeguard's rescuing,
         Water splashing,
           People swimming,
             Boy's walking,
               Girl's going,
                 Wind blowing,
                   It's cold!

Jennifer Maddock (9)
St Margaret's CE Junior School, Newcastle-under-Lyme

STONE DEAD

She waits for her prey
in a dark lonely cave.
Slithering, scaly snakes upon her head
big bulging scary eyes
that pierce through your soul.
Long bloodstained yellow teeth
venomous snakes sprouting
and tusks that come from her mouth.

Once those snakes used to be hair.
Long, black and beautiful.
Soft red skin that's no longer there.
Blue sparkling eyes that no one could resist.
Now it's all gone.
She only has a croaky voice
and pulling eyes that hypnotise you
into stone!

Rachel Hancock (10)
St Margaret's CE Junior School, Newcastle-under-Lyme

THE SEA

The sea is like a slithering snake.
It lies in wait
for its big break
when the sea is calm
it doesn't hurt a fly.
When the waves are coming
you go running!
Because its mouth is open wide
the only thing a snake cannot do
is stretch for miles and miles.

Rebecca Goddard (8)
St Margaret's CE Junior School, Newcastle-under-Lyme

THE SEA

When I think of the sea these are the words
that come to me.
Water and waves, fishes and shells.
Seaweed, pebbles and funny smells.
The sea so deep and oceans blue.
Seagulls around - what view!
I think of holidays, having fun
playing with Rosie in the sun.
Swimming in the sea
paddling in our boat.
Daddy holds us tight on a long rope.
Sitting on the beach, eating ice-creams.
Will it soon be bedtime?
Was it all a dream?

Katie Stanway (8)
St Margaret's CE Junior School, Newcastle-under-Lyme

MY HAMSTERS NAME IS NIBBLES

My hamsters name is Nibbles
she bites me all the time.
She runs around and around until she has to stop.
She squeaks and squeaks and squeaks until I get annoyed.
I put some food by her bed
she's fairly fat indeed.
When it's dark for her to see, she eats and runs and drinks.
She lets me stroke her in her cage, she does not bite me then
and if she's in a moody mood - I leave her where she is.

Kate Tarpey (9)
St Margaret's CE Junior School, Newcastle-under-Lyme

MY DOG

I have a dog called Josh
I took him for a walk.
He saw a pretty poodle
And thought she was very posh.

I took my dog to the park
But he began to bark.
Then I suddenly realised
He was barking at a lark.

My dog said to himself
'I really want a bone,
But my master won't let me
Because she'll have to get a loan.'

My dog is insane
So we took him to the vets
And the X-ray showed
He hasn't got a brain.

In memory of my dog Josh!

Stevie Saponja (8)
St Margaret's CE Junior School, Newcastle-under-Lyme

THE SEA

The sea is like a horse
running up and down the shore
and when he runs away - he's scared
and when he's calm - he's asleep
and when he plays gently
children play with him.

Amber Allen (8)
St Margaret's CE Junior School, Newcastle-under-Lyme

SUMMER

Bluebell's drooping

People burning

Tulip's dancing

Children splashing

Duck's quacking

Toddler's smiling.

Mum's groaning

Dad's moaning

Sunflower's opening

Shop's closing

Long days and short nights.

Wake up in the morning
and start another day.

Charlotte Kerr (9)
St Margaret's CE Junior School, Newcastle-under-Lyme

SWIMMING

People splashing
People swimming
Toddler's pacing
Mum's relaxing
Bully's ducking
Children sliding

Arm's thrashing
Jessie's winning
Teenager's racing
Dad's floating
Lifeguard saving
It's smashing

Splashing . . .

Lauren Bailey (8)
St Margaret's CE Junior School, Newcastle-under-Lyme

I LOVE MY DOG JESS

I love my dog Jess
who is the best dog in the world.
I love my dog Jess
who is very cheeky.

I love my dog Jess
who slobbers all over her toys.
I love my dog Jess
who is very lazy.

I love my dog Jess
who is beautiful.
I love my dog Jess
who sits with her chin up
just like a queen.

Eve Funnell (8)
St Margaret's CE Junior School, Newcastle-under-Lyme

PLAYING IN THE WATER

Children splashing
Wave's slashing
Swimmer's dashing
Bodies clashing
Temper's flashing
Boy's bashing
Arm's lashing
Teeth gnashing
It's smashing . . .

Phoebe Sparrow (8)
St Margaret's CE Junior School, Newcastle-under-Lyme

THE SEA AND WAVES

The sea and the waves rushing by
all the fish are very shy.
The howling wolf is beating it
and the sea is pushing it
as it goes on, it makes a terrible roar.
Then the sun comes out
and makes a beating tune.
As the day goes on you will see
the reflecting moon.

If you go to see the sea
and listen to the sounds.
The sea going to and fro.
Do you know the sound of the sea?
Because I know.

Emily Worrall (9)
St Margaret's CE Junior School, Newcastle-under-Lyme

DEEP IN THE FOREST

Deep in the forest where it's damp and dark.
I wish I was at home - playing in the park.
Trees are blowing from side to side
I'm looking at the way all the bird's glide.
My mum shouted me
'It's time to go'
and then I saw a cheetah shoot by.
I looked at my shoes below
how dirty and muddy they were.
Then it was really time to go
so I went home and relaxed.

Leanne Ray (9)
St Margaret's CE Junior School, Newcastle-under-Lyme

APOCALYPSE

An atmosphere is gloomy
The world it's prey awaits
Satan's battle is starting.
The world will just have to wait.

Clouds now dark
Acid will fall.
Life on earth is nothing
Nothing at all.

The mists are moving
Graves and corpses it leaves.
Light now shines on a single spot.
The child from earth is born.

Duncan McNeil (11)
St Margaret's CE Junior School, Newcastle-under-Lyme

AEROPLANES

Everybody rushing so they get there on time.
Aeroplanes food like slime
All children sleeping
Engine's bleeping
Captain's busy
People get dizzy
Seat belts clopping
Ear's popping
Robbie Williams on a private jet.

Lee Hughes (9)
St Margaret's CE Junior School, Newcastle-under-Lyme

THE OLD AND THE NEW

I hate being like this.
Imagine having hair that makes a hiss.
Once I was beautiful
with long black hair
and now I've got grizzly snakes
which no one would like to wear.

My powerful eyes of deep dark red
beautiful blue ones I should have instead.
I wait in the corner
for something to eat.
Whenever I've killed them - I eat their meat.

I used to have beautiful white teeth
and now they're black and as long as grief.
A cave is my house
As dark as the night.
With no little peep of beautiful sunlight.

Amy Johnson (10)
St Margaret's CE Junior School, Newcastle-under-Lyme

THE SEA

The sea is like a lion
roaring wild and strong.
It runs for miles and miles
singing its roaring song.
Sometimes it's calm and quiet and free.
It seems like it's watching me
when I'm on the beach.
The lion goes quietly out of reach.

Matthew Cotton (9)
St Margaret's CE Junior School, Newcastle-under-Lyme

My Pet Mouse

I have a pet mouse, I call him
Squeeze.
He eats lots and lots and lots of
cheese.
He runs around the house at night
just to give my mum a fright.
He hides in corners or on the stairs
to catch my mum so unawares.
She screams and shouts and runs
about.
'Do something someone - get it out!'
I run downstairs and grab him
quick.
'I've got him mum - don't have a
fit.'
He only wants a little piece
of that cheese you brought from
Greece.
So don't be cross, don't be mean
make my mouse's life a dream.
Just a little bit of cheese,
for my favourite pet called Squeeze.

Emma Walker (10)
St Margaret's CE Junior School, Newcastle-under-Lyme

Colours

Red is the colour of roses.
Yellow is the sun.
Green is the leaves on a beautiful sunny day.
Black is dark and scary.
Brown is the burning of wood.

Stephen Barrs (9)
St Margaret's CE Junior School, Newcastle-under-Lyme

ONCE A BEAUTY - NOW LOST

Where once flowing black curls were
there are spitting, swirling, slimy green snakes
curling, whirling - everywhere.

Where eyes were big and shining blue
now they're jealous, red and yellow.
Cruel and sharp, sore
bloodshot and hateful.

She will take your life away
in one quick glance.
Her breath is vile
she won't need to look at you.
It will leave you
gasping for breath.

Lucy S Street (10)
St Margaret's CE Junior School, Newcastle-under-Lyme

THE TREE

It's like a human hand
reaching up to grab its fortune.
It has a sparkling green glove on
but when the weather becomes colder
it changes into a golden sheet.
The snow starts to fall and the
golden sheet is blown off so all
that is left is the spooky bare hands.

Gradually after many years
the hands become gnarled and diseased.
Until they sadly disintegrate and die.

Rachel Millward (10)
St Margaret's CE Junior School, Newcastle-under-Lyme

FOG

The fog slithered silently and
stealthily across the weeping field,
engulfing everything in its
treacherous path.

Houses cried and shouted for help
as he swallowed them in his ugly
smelly mouth angrily shouting
for more.

Children ran crying home
shouting for their mothers.
But the icy glare of the fog
catches them, freezes them.

Suddenly he slithered away,
only to come another wet
and terrible day.

Alex Pardoe (11)
St Margaret's CE Junior School, Newcastle-under-Lyme

WATER

Water, water - I love you.
Splashing, crashing, smashing
rushing down a mountain
and swimming in the sea.
Now I have to go
but I'll be back.

Gregory Braddick (8)
St Margaret's CE Junior School, Newcastle-under-Lyme

MEDUSA'S LAIR

In Medusa's lair
with her hissing hair
there is no end to the night
Medusa's face is a dreadful sight.

Medusa's hissing hair . . .
Snakes are slithering everywhere.
It's all stone statues - nothing there!
She lost her beauty
She does not care.

In a stone valley
outside her lair.
She waits for people to enter.
No one did
until the day -
his name was Perseus.

Now Medusa's dead
Perseus chopped off her head.
He chopped it off with one big whack.
He's taken it back to his pride-land
where he will turn the king to stone.

Daniel Parker (9)
St Margaret's CE Junior School, Newcastle-under-Lyme

THE HORRID HEAD

The lonely and the jealous.
The fearful and the ugly
That's Medusa!

Powerful and aggressive.
Barbaric
Killer of children - with a stare of stone.
Medusa hisses, it's not fair.

Medusa's stench!
The stench of death
The venomous spray in the smelly air
The knockout gas from her hair.
The only master in this dry, dry land
is the spray of venom.

Stuart Kelly (9)
St Margaret's CE Junior School, Newcastle-under-Lyme

MUTATED MEDUSA

When Medusa was mutated
her only loss was beauty and love.
Now she's only angry
because she's kept her wickedness
and lost her beauty and love.

Icy breath, hissing hair
now she's mutated.
Nobody's there
because she's so ugly.

Bloodshot eyes
so hypnotic.
One look and when you're
spotted by Medusa
there's no chance
of getting away.

There's something scary about her eyes
deadly, scary and a killer.
One look and you're turned to stone
forever . . .

Philip Jolley (9)
St Margaret's CE Junior School, Newcastle-under-Lyme

THE GHOSTS

The ghosts are coming tonight, tonight.
The ghosts are coming tonight.

Out of the forest
on nimble feet
across the gully
and down the street.

The ghosts are coming tonight.

They sniff at the moon
with short, sharp noses.
Come into the gardens
and sniff the roses.

The ghosts are coming tonight.

They walk on roofs
and on the floors.
Look in the windows
and shake the doors.

The ghosts are coming tonight.

The children are tight in their beds.
Tight with fright and fear.

Laura Burgess (10)
St Margaret's CE Junior School, Newcastle-under-Lyme

ANIMALS

I went to the pet shop with my mum
bought a dog and went away.
Came home from school and saw the dog
playing in the garden with a hedgehog.
So I went to get a rabbit
but it had a hoppity habit.
I swapped the rabbit for a snake
then it slid into the lake.
So I picked up a little rat.
Bit me! So I got a cat.
The cat was mean and sat on a log
not to mention my cute little dog.

Sophie Wood (9)
St Margaret's CE Junior School, Newcastle-under-Lyme

NIGHT HORSE

Night horse, night horse
run through the night.
Don't stop on your way
or you'll get a fright.
Run passed the trees
with the shadows on the floor.
Gallop, gallop
to your stable door.

Alexandra Powney (8)
St Margaret's CE Junior School, Newcastle-under-Lyme

SUMMER

Summertime has come
children play outside.
Playing out till summer ends
playing on the slide.

Go out to the seaside.
Waves are rushing by
playing with your beach ball
bucket and spade and sand.

Beautiful flowers
are growing in the garden.
Tulips and blossom.
Blossom - pink and white.
Tulips are bright red.

Lovely flowers
purple and green.
Red, blue and orange.

Summer has ended.
Autumn has come
leaves are falling
off the trees.

Charlotte Weller (9)
St Margaret's CE Junior School, Newcastle-under-Lyme

PLAYING OUTSIDE

Playing outside with my friends
doing cartwheels and backbends.
Running round, falling on the ground.
Running our fingers through the sand.
I fall and I then begin to cry.
My mum has got a lot of sympathy.
Yes, for me!
We then go home - we're really tired
then we go to bed
with our sleepy heads.
Then rise and shine
we're out of our bed.

Janine Larkin (8)
St Margaret's CE Junior School, Newcastle-under-Lyme

SEASIDE

With the lovely sunshine
on the tropical beach.
I go into the sea
where sharks are approaching me.
So I get out of the sea
and say 'Where's my beach ball gone?'
And then a crab comes by with the beach ball
in its pincers and nips my toe
and I say 'Ow!'
And that's it from the tropical beach
'Wow!'

Iain Hope (8)
St Margaret's CE Junior School, Newcastle-under-Lyme

THE FLOWERS

Growing plants.
Bird's eating seeds.
The sun is shining
like a beautiful candle.
The grass is shining as well.
Bird's singing in the trees.
Flowers swaying
side to side.

Bruce Halliwell (8)
St Margaret's CE Junior School, Newcastle-under-Lyme

FEAR

Red is the colour of fiery hot flames.
It tastes like hot chilly powder burning
in my mouth.
It smells like burning wood.
It looks like mighty flames.
Sounds like strong winds blowing.
It feels like the sun's powerful rays.

Sam Massey (8)
St Margaret's CE Junior School, Newcastle-under-Lyme

WITCHCRAFT

Once upon a time in a faraway land
across the deserts and far from sand.
Lived in a castle a very mean witch
with a nose like a peg and fingers that snitch.
But now we move to another room
just the same but a different ghoul.

And downstairs in her dungeon
are the bottles with poison.
In her spell-room with all her rats
and also her pet cats.

Anthony Zobkiw (9)
St Margaret's CE Junior School, Newcastle-under-Lyme

A SILENT DEATH

It's silent there in that cave
a stone stave sits waiting
hissing all over its head.
With one look you're dead - stone dead!
Snakes curling, hissing, spitting all over the place
she can kill with just her face.
Stone statues stuck there with a look of horror
implanted on their faces.
Her huge curled, twisted ivory tusks
match her bloodstained yellow teeth.

She's lonely there with her hypnotic stare.
No one to talk to.
Except the stone statues.
A lost beauty she wants so much back.
She wasted it - it's her fault.
She was so mean.
Now she can't even be seen
by the human eye without turning them to stone.
She misses her black curls, her smooth face,
could anyone solve her case?

Toby Plant (10)
St Margaret's CE Junior School, Newcastle-under-Lyme

THE MAGIC BOX

I will put in the box
the ticking of my clock.
The weeks going past.
The speech of my grandad.

I will put in my box
secrets of my life.
The days I won't have again
the steps I took.

I will put in my box
my football goals.
My swimming strokes
the memories.

I will put in my box
my old wrestling people
and their old songs.
Their memories of when they won.

My box is fashioned from
steel, iron, money
with stars on top
and rubies and diamonds.

I will surf in my box
to a tropical island.

Robert Standell (10)
St Mary's RC Primary School, Leek

THE MAGIC BOX

I will put in the box
the cheekiness of my kitten's crying.
All my favourite memories to keep
and look back on.
The noise of the waves in seashells.

I will put in the box
all my friend's smiling and smirking faces.
The laughter of my sisters.
My great aunt smiling and
laughing joyfully.

I will put in the box
my precious memories,
my secrets to share.
My kitten's long tabby hair
and the colour of my aunt's eyes.

Tawny Hill (10)
St Mary's RC Primary School, Leek

LIMERICKS

There was a young lady of Lynn
who was so uncommonly thin
that when she essayed
to drink lemonade
she slipped through the straw
and fell in.

Vu Anh Nguyen (10)
St Mary's RC Primary School, Leek

LIMERICKS

There was a young lady called Em
who picked bunches of flowers by their stem.
She started to wheeze
then did a big sneeze.
One by one all of those flowers
she dropped them.

Emma Carter (11)
St Mary's RC Primary School, Leek

THE MAN FROM DUNDEE

There was an old man from Dundee,
he lived in a van by the sea.
He lived at the end of the street
his name was Pete.
He saw a flea and went back to Dundee.

Benjamin Field (10)
St Mary's RC Primary School, Leek

FLYING

It felt so good to fly.
To be up there in the sky.
Flying around
With no feet on the ground.
Oh what fun to be so high!

Samuel Henry Hunt (10)
St Mary's RC Primary School, Leek

THE MAGIC BOX

I will put in the box . . .

The purring of a polar bear on a peaceful night.
The flame of a flickering fire.
The sound of Atiwin's voice in Ghana.

I will put in the box . . .

Bubbles bouncing on the waves.
The sunset setting on the sea.
The smile on everyone's face
when they smile.

I will put in the box . . .

The sound of Pip squeaking sorrowfully.
The sun shining brightly.
The noise of a monster growling.

I will put in the box . . .

All of my memories.
My grandparents speaking to me.
And seven thousand pounds.

My box is fashioned from gold and rubies
with stars on the lid and dolphins
in the corners.
Its hinges are made of dragon's teeth.

I shall drink in my box
a flaming volcano made of lava
and taste in my mouth - a volcano erupting.

Elizabeth Sillito (11)
St Mary's RC Primary School, Leek

INTO THE SEA

I dived into the sea
where the sharks never go
at the bed of a quill at
the bottom of the ocean.
Down, down I fell to the ground
like falling off a mountain
with no air above or below me
but sea.
I swam through the seaweed
and listened to the oysters
at my feet.

Cassie Bratt
St Mary's RC Primary School, Leek

THE FAIRY'S HOUR

Fairies, fairies fly around
fly upon this golden ground
fly where only fairy magic
can be seen.
Fairy magic falls down
when fairies float around.
They float up and down.
Right above the
golden ground.

Anna Niebieska (10)
St Mary's RC Primary School, Leek

DRAGON FIRE

Emerald trees stretch out their beautiful branches
feeling mighty proud.
The dragon awakes in a fiery rage
hungry for the sight of food.
An amber mist appears
as the fire sweeps through the wood.
Scorching hot scaly skin
fierce flickering flames within.
The moon seems to shimmer way up high
in the golden misty sky.
The awful smell of smoke
causes ghastly choking.
The dragon takes a luscious bite -
leaving only charred remains of the once
beautiful forest.

Lorna Poole (10) Elisa Etemad (10)
Christina Wallace (10) Abigail Hall (9)
Marianne King (10)
St Thomas's RC Primary School, Tean

GHOSTS AND VAMPIRES

Ghosts and vampires
with foul smelling breath
caused a fire
scaring everybody to death.

Alex Humphries (9)
St Thomas's RC Primary School, Tean

DISTURBED

A hot tempered dragon awakens
from his slumber.
The smell of smoke awakens the forest.
Scorching fierce flames skipping
between the trees.
Burning wood, crackling, spitting.
Dragon terrorises all.
A hundred voices screaming between
the trees.
The hot tempered dragon cools down
slowly.
Wood embers glow in the quiet of the
night.

Silence.

Lee Wood (10) John Finnegan (11)
Dale Tunstall (11) Liam Forristal (11)
Grant Ravenscroft (10)
St Thomas's RC Primary School, Tean

THE ANGRY DRAGON

The fire is an angry dragon waiting
in the forest.
Sharp spikes on his back
licking the trees around him.
Tree trunks alight with scorching flames.
Trees burning
Flames that bring death to all nature.

Branches crack and crash to the ground.
The crackle and roar of the spitting fire
flaming nostrils pouring out smoke.
Violent flames rush.

Oonagh Scannell (9) Amy Burgoyne (9)
Natasha Hallam (10) Judith Downie (10)
Luke Dalkin
St Thomas's RC Primary School, Tean

FOREST FIRE

Gigantic flames dance in the twilight
an acrid smell lingers in the atmosphere.
The furious dragon rampages through
scorching embers.
'You're next!' he commands abruptly.
Horrified trees huddle close together
fighting for their lives.
Branches vanish as the sizzling fire darts past
smoke coming from every direction
engulfs the lungs of petrified creatures.
The fire destroys everything in its path.
Cinders crunch under its heavy feet.
Tired and sleepy he continues his slumber.
Now like a startled fawn
He softly snores.

Sophie Whieldon (11) Caroline Darley (11)
Mark Mogadam (11) Jessica Darley (11)
Emma Walford (11)
St Thomas's RC Primary School, Tean

MASTER OF DESTRUCTION

Hot tempered dragon waking with thoughts
of destruction.
Gradually igniting his first fierce flames
with rage.
Embers falling through choking smoke.
Dead creatures trailing in his path.
The vile smell of burning flesh choking
any living thing.
His blistering red and yellow blaze
lighting the morning fog.
With echoes of spits, crackles and
rustles in the burnt bushes.

Yan Pavlovic (11) Robert Smith (11)
Samuel Worthington (11) Kristian Finney (10)
Adam Layland (11)
St Thomas's RC Primary School, Tean

THE FIRE-BREATHING DRAGON

Sweltering, sizzling eyes staring from every direction.
Vile smells coming from his steaming breath.
Explosions banging from his red-hot fire
at every second, killing a part of nature.
His rough scaly skin is impossible to touch.
Spiky flames spitting at trees, making them lifeless.
Steaming red-hot eyes glaring every second
he sees nature arrive and nature destroyed.
Still roaring and growling.
Yelling
'I am the ruler of the Universe!'

Laura Marsh (11) Heather Deaville (10)
Kirsty Shotton (10) Kelly Rushton (10)
Lindsay Withington (11)
St Thomas's RC Primary School, Tean

A KITTEN

A kitten is a small army-man on a mission
to find his food with a hungry look upon
his face.

A kitten is a silky jumper soft against your
skin.
A kitten is a tiny lion ripping and tearing
your belongings.
A kitten is a playful child trying to amuse
itself.
A kitten is a ball of snow, tumbling and
falling on the ground.
A kitten is a tiger walking through the jungle
with different colours and findings.
A kitten is a ball of wool stretching across
the floor.

Megan Wilson (11)
Springvale County Primary School

THE MOON

The moon is a dark, dull beach ball
The moon is a kite rising in the air.
The moon is a firework just about to take off.
The moon is a basketball shooting in the tall net.
The moon is a dark blue balloon swaying up high.
The moon is a huge star in the dark, dark sky.
The moon is a big, green dinghy.
The moon is a baseball just being hit by a bat.

Richard Woolley (10)
Springvale County Primary School

ASSEMBLY

At five past nine we line up at the door.
'Oh no! It's assembly time!'
People start to fidget and whisper 'Here's the bore!'
He shouts - it's not as if we've committed a crime.

He starts the same old story
the one about how to stop headlice.
It's never violent, exciting or gory
people start to gossip as quiet as mice.

Finally it's finished, our punishment is done.
Let's go and find a four-leaf clover
and try and have some fun
now that boring assembly is over.

Let's hope the clover will bring us luck
because I hate assembly - it sucks.

Natasha Wilton (11)
Springvale County Primary School

WATER

Rivers rushing down the stream,
Drinking water's very clean,
Waterfalls come gushing down,
Shoot a water pistol like a clown.

Loch Ness is really big,
Me and my dad play water tig,
Fishes swim really fast,
Pirates always shout 'Avast!'

Joseph Apperley (10)
Springvale County Primary School

HORSES

Horses are very fast,
They live now but also in the past,
They eat bran grass and hay,
They gallop about every day.

Horses are very posh,
And cost a lot of dosh,
You have to feed and clean them,
As well as beautifully treat them.

They gallop as fast as a car,
And they travel very far,
They like me and you,
And they do anything we want them to do.

Natalie Jones (9)
Springvale County Primary School

MINEHEAD

Minehead is very sunny
the entertainment is very funny.
The hotels are very posh
and I said to my mum
'Have you got any dosh?'
I asked for a lift to town
and the man only said it went down.
We went to the beach
and got as rosy as a peach.
So I went for a dip in the sea
and the waves splashed
all over me.

James Poynton (9)
Springvale County Primary School

FLOWERS

Flowers, flowers, I love flowers.
Tulips, daisies they grow all hours.
They grow in parks, fields and towers,
So that we can gaze at them for many hours.

My favourite flowers are tulips,
they look like colourful egg cups,
colourful egg cups they are.
On a rainy day
they are lovely to play.
Animals live in little flowers.

Bees collect the pollen and make it into honey.
Bunnies jump around
and jump all around.
Daffodils are yellow,
hello little fellow.
Make it into a cello.
Flowers grow in summer
Sing a song like a drummer.
Daffodils, as white as summer.

Lauren Butler (9)
Springvale County Primary School

SPRING

When the days are getting warmer,
And the nights are getting lighter,
Flowers and leaves begin to sprout,
Longer days mean you can play outside,
And the fruit blossom starts to grow.

Adam Heath (10)
Springvale County Primary School

A CAT IS...

A cat is a hot water bottle
keeping you warm when you're ill.

A cat is a selfish toddler
always squawking for attention.

A cat is a tyrant, hardly ever forgiving
and often the cause of pain.

A cat is a little rascal
always up to mischief and being naughty.

A cat is a friend
always there for you when you're sad.

Kristina Fisher (11)
Springvale County Primary School

WHAT IS A BED?

A bed is a soft beach of sand
covered by the pale blue sea.

A bed is a dreamland of sleeping
dwarfs, snoring loudly.

It is a sofa bouncing up and down
when you jump onto it.

A bed is a panda, soft and cuddly,
waiting for you to give it a big hug.

It is a mouse, really quiet but very squeaky,
especially when the springs break.

Terri Lea Bentley (10)
Springvale County Primary School

BASKETBALL

A basketball is a grasshopper jumping up and down,
getting closer and closer to its goal.
Hopping over fences and leaping onto walls.
Pushed by a beetle, he ends up in the other side of the garden.
Starting again, a thrush catches him in his beak
and drops him down a burrow.

Julian Bishop (11)
Springvale County Primary School

THE PRISONER

I wish I could run away
I cannot face another day
I dream of home and the sun
I just want to run and run
I miss my loving family
I just wish I wasn't in agony.

Lisa Bate (10)
Springvale County Primary School

THE SEA

A stormy night on the sea,
see the water,
clashing and bashing
up the rocks
smashing a ship
into smithereens.

Adam Penhorwood (10)
Springvale County Primary School

WHAT IS A BASEBALL?

A baseball is an asteroid flying through outer space.
It is the sun flying through the air and blazing brightly.
It is the icy snowball which is being thrown.
It is a face constantly looking straight at you.
It is a planet in space which is floating around.
It is a shooting star whooshing across the dark night sky.
It is an island floating across the deep blue sea.
It is a globe spinning around and revealing various
names of the countries.

Alfie Poynton (10)
Springvale County Primary School

THE DAY NEVER ENDS

As the sun rises,
we all wake
Although the sun doesn't rise,
the earth rotates.

It takes 24 hours
and when we reach the other side
We're in darkness, we call it night,
but day is still alive.

Day never ends,
the sun never goes down
it's just the earth
going round and round.

Rebecca Bishop (11)
Stoneydelph Junior School

MILLENNIUM 2000

It's nearly here
It's nearly coming
It's really big
It's massive
What is?
The Millennium 2000
Of course.
It's going too slow
It's going too fast
Come on
Come on
Hurry,
Hurry up.
It's the night
It's hear.
I'm so excited
We danced all night.
We had a great time
Ding, dong
Happy New Year
They all kiss.
They get into a circle
They sing a little song
We stayed until 4 o'clock
Goodbye, goodbye.

Lauren Johnston (10)
Tillington Manor Primary School

FOOTBALL

The perfect day, the perfect day
I would like this day to stay.
Got signed by Man United
And earning 10,000 pounds a day.

The perfect day, the perfect day
The transfer I completed, I'm on my way.
I've seen Old Trafford in my dreams
And now I am here at the Theatre of Dreams.

The perfect day, the perfect day
I am on the pitch about to play,
My family is watching, I have scored
And all the crowd greatly applaud.

The perfect day, the perfect day
I am in the second match and about to play.
I am playing Leeds United, beating them *hooray!*
And all this is my perfect day.

Scott Hall (10)
Tillington Manor Primary School

ANIMALS IN THE WINTER

In the winter the animals make a home.
Then go into bed and pretend to be dead
They sleep all through winter and do not wake up at a noise
But did you know they only wake up in spring?

Soibhian Knight (10)
Tillington Manor Primary School

SCHOOL

Handwriting, boring
Neat work.

Shut up
No sound.

Quiet class
No noise.

Everyone working
Pin dropped.

Bell goes
Classroom's clear.

Jamie Cartwright (10)
Tillington Manor Primary School

RIVERS

Crashing, slashing at the sides
boats are bobbing bow to bow
If the rainpour is very good
we're surely going to have a flood.

Rapidly dashing down the river
it sometimes makes fishermen quiver
eventually nearly at the sea
all of that water *Yippee! Yippee!*
Little children swimming there
rubbish and litter everywhere
hardly anybody gives a care
because the people love it there.

Aaron Nixon (11)
William Shrewsbury Primary School

THE RIVER'S JOURNEY

Rivers flow, firm and fast,
Until they reach the sea at last,
As the raindrop hits the ground,
It makes a sort of splashing sound.

As the river flows about,
It twists and shimmers, full of trout,
After erosion starts to wear,
A year goes, it's hardly there.

Twisting, turning on its way,
It moves about in a kind of sway,
On its journey to the sea,
It flows along with joyful glee.

Michael Duddy (11)
William Shrewsbury Primary School

IN SEARCH OF THE SEA

Water cascades down the waterfall, with salmon leaping
The water shimmers and glitters in the sun
It meanders round the corner in search for the sea.
The river's getting to the sea
There's seaweed bobbing by
Here come the waves rippling up the river
The huge waves smashing on the shore
As the river meanders once more
The river rushes down to the beach to the sea.

Johnathan Armstrong (10)
William Shrewsbury Primary School

THE RIVER'S JOURNEY

Trickling down the hillside, a shimmering little thing.
Darting around the rocks and pebbles washing them all clean.
The whirlpools are whirling round so fast that tiny sparkling
droplets are floating past.

Sheep are grazing in a nearby field.
Crumbling houses and ancient castles stand close to the narrow bank.
A deer and its fawn huddle together under a large clump of trees.

The river curves and tumbles through steep gorges,
whizzing and whirling past forests,
white, bubbling foam gathers around the edges.

The river, a deep sapphire blue colour winds it way
down the countryside and loops in the small town of Caymorth.
The channel of water curves under a low arching bridge.
A small child stands throwing stones into the river.

The grassy banks are sprinkled with people
having picnics and enjoying the summer sun.
Swans glide in the slow moving current, swooping
for bread that the passers-by throw in.

Golden leaves sail down the bumpy rapids,
Iris sway in the gentle breeze.
Splish, splash, splosh! Where has it gone?
Now in the city, roaring noisily, it's gone down, down and under,
slipping through its narrow gorge then spilling out, no longer smooth.

Through the backstreets tumbling and turning
in its narrow channel - yearning for the sea.
A lamp light flickers as the river dodges in and out.

Night falls and the dark wide river makes its way to the sea in darkness.
The sun breaks free and we're at the sea, white seagulls are squealing
and wheeling high.

Jewelled sandy beaches are splattered in red, green, blue, yellow
and purple towels.
People are enjoying the hot summer sun, the river's reached
its destination, tired but happy it floats away under the light blue sky,
ready for another day.

Charlotte Nutland (11)
William Shrewsbury Primary School

WATERFALL

Waterfall
cascades over the rocks
Hurling itself down the edge
eroding the rocks as it falls.
Gets faster as it descends
gliding near the end.

Splash!

Jamie Sandells (10)
William Shrewsbury Primary School

WATERFALL

As the water gets to a waterfall,
It crashes and splashes, zooms and booms,
Getting faster and faster as it falls,
Then it reaches the bottom,
And you hear an almighty
Splash!

Ben Watson (11)
William Shrewsbury Primary School

THE RIVER

The river swirling, curling, twisting as it slowly flows downstream,
getting faster, swifter, rushing, gushing, pouring down the hill.
Slowing down, lingering, sluggishly sweeping over rocks,
eroding banks, depositing mud, carrying stones, catching raindrops,
A curling, swirling, twisting river approaching the blue shimmering sea.

Sophie Horner (10)
William Shrewsbury Primary School

RIVERS

A cold winter day,
    When the river was flowing,
        the ducks were swimming.
            Along by the riverside,
                and the flowers were blooming.

Stacey Smith (11)
William Shrewsbury Primary School

RIVERS

Down by the river.
Erosion beating the side.
The mud deposits.
Meander gets more twisty,
It is going to the sea.

Andrew Lamb (10)
William Shrewsbury Primary School

RAINDROP'S JOURNEY

The clouds, saturated,
The rain falls down,
It lands in the river,
It twists and turns,
When will it end?
It seems to go on forever.

It disappears in the mountains,
Then meanders right out,
Keeps on cascading,
It's never-ending,
Splashes and sploshes,
Plishes and ploshes,
Especially when it hits some rocks.

The choppy water,
Becomes faster and faster,
It slaps on the walls,
Tearing the rocks away,
It becomes murkier and murkier,
Its journey's coming to an end,
As it swirls through the estuary,
It calms down now,
As it lands in the cool sea.

Sophie Partridge (10)
William Shrewsbury Primary School